STUDIES IN JOSEPHUS

STUDIES IN JOSEPHUS

R. J. H. SHUTT
M.A., Ph.D. (Durham)
Lazenby Chaplain, University of Exeter

LONDON
S·P·C·K
1961

First published in 1961
by S.P.C.K.
Holy Trinity Church
Marylebone Road
London N.W.1

Made and printed in Great Britain by
William Clowes and Sons, Limited, London and Beccles

This book is dedicated as a small affectionate tribute
to the memory of the late

GEORGE CHATTERTON RICHARDS, D.D.,

Priest, Canon of Durham, and Professor of Greek
and Classical Literature in the University of
Durham, under whose inspiring tutorship this
research work began, and by whose scholarship,
so freely imparted, developed into an interest
which has increased over the years.

R. I. P.

CONTENTS

PREFACE

D R FOAKES JACKSON's book, entitled *Josephus and the Jews*,[1] was published in 1930. As its sub-title explains, it was intended to investigate "the religion and history of the Jews as explained by Flavius Josephus." Its conclusion is[2] as follows: "In a word, Josephus is not a dead author, but is still alive with a message for this generation."

At that time, a considerable amount of work on Josephus had been done by Dr Thackeray, whose lectures entitled *Josephus the Man and the Historian*[3] appeared in 1929. He was also editor of the editon of Josephus in the Loeb series: the *War*, the *Life*, and *Contra Apionem* had already appeared, and in 1930 the first volume of the *Jewish Antiquities* in that series was published. The first part of his *Lexicon to Josephus*[4] appeared in 1930, to be followed in 1934 by the second.[5] When Dr Thackeray died in 1930, his work was continued by Dr Marcus.

Except for parts of the *Lexicon* and volumes in the Loeb series, the amount published on Josephus since 1930 is small, and if the claim is true that "Josephus is not a dead author but is still alive", this book may perhaps be justified.

In Dr Foakes Jackson's book, particular attention is paid to the content of Josephus' works. In these studies, the emphasis is rather upon the language of Josephus, and its attendant problems. This trend towards the emphasis upon Josephus' language is discernible in the *Lexicon*, part of which Dr Thackeray prepared, and it is probable that in this way further light can be thrown upon the problems set for us by

---

[1] S.P.C.K. [2] Intro., p. xvi.
[3] New York: Jewish Institute of Religion Press.
[4] Paris.
[5] Part 3 published in 1948; Part 4 in 1955.

Josephus as a man and as a historian. It is easy to expect too much from this approach, and such a danger needs to be recognized: nevertheless if this book establishes the need for the study of the language of Josephus as part of the whole field which is to be covered, it will have achieved at least part of its purpose.

The first chapter gives brief accounts of Josephus' life and works, so as to make clear his environment, expressed intentions, and underlying principles with regard to his historical writing. Chapters on the *Jewish War* and the *Contra Apionem* follow. Two chapters are devoted to the *Jewish Antiquities*: the first of these (chapter 4) refers especially to Josephus' assistants and the way in which their assistance was given; the second (chapter 5) investigates the style of Josephus with special reference to Nicolaus of Damascus, Dionysius of Halicarnassus, Polybius, and Strabo.

The account of the editions and texts of Josephus in chapter 6 is intended to show the trends in the study of Josephus up to the present time.

Finally, an estimate is made of the character of the author and the value of his works, in the light of his own avowed intentions mentioned in the first chapter and the investigations carried out in the intervening chapters.

CHAPTER I

JOSEPHUS
His Life and Writings

JOSEPHUS was born "in the first year of the reign of
Gaius Caesar",[1] that is, between A.D. 37 and 38. He was
proud of his family,[2] and gives a full account of his family
tree as described in the public records.[3] "I am", he says,
"not only sprung from the sacerdotal family in general, but
from the first of the twenty-four courses."[4] Moreover, he was
of the chief family of the first course also, and by his mother
the royal blood of the Asmoneans flowed in his veins.[4] His
great-grandfather, Simon Psellus, was a contemporary of
Simon Hyrcanus the High Priest,[5] and his father's name was
Matthias, to whose nobility and righteousness he proudly
points as qualifications for eminence.[6]

Josephus himself had three sons,[7] Hyrcanus, Justus, and
Agrippa. He received his education with his brother Matthias,
and we may presume that it was the best education available
for the son of a priest, and would include instruction in the
Law by learned rabbis. His mother tongue was Aramaic.
Josephus was a promising pupil and soon outstripped his
brother.[8] His love of learning was so outstanding that he was
consulted by the chief priests and principal men of the city
when he was only fourteen years old.[9]

In A.D. 53, when he was sixteen, it became necessary for him
to decide to belong to the sect of the Pharisees, the Sadducees,
or the Essenes;[10] he took the unusual but sensible step of trying

[1] *Life* 5 (Whiston's translation). [2] *Contra Ap.* I. 54.
[3] *Life* 6. [4] Ibid. 2. [5] Ibid. 3.
[6] Ibid. 7. [7] Ibid. 5. [8] Ibid. 8.
[9] Ibid. 9. [10] Ibid. 10.

each one first before making his decision. The days of testing involved hardship and discipline, and his account of the sects[1] testifies to his thoroughness. Even so, he was not satisfied, and joined for a time a certain Banus,[2] who lived a strict ascetic life, probably according to Essene ideals. All this took him three years,[3] after which on his return to Jerusalem he attached himself to the Pharisees.

There is no record of his activities for the next seven years of his life, which he spent quietly performing his duties as a priest in Jerusalem. But he became during this time well known among his immediate associates. "After the twenty-sixth year of his life"[4] an incident occurred which brought him into prominence and had a profound and lasting influence upon him. Felix the Procurator had imprisoned some of his fellow priests on a trifling charge, and sent them to Rome to appear before Caesar. Either officially or unofficially Josephus became their champion and worked hard to secure their release. It meant a journey to Rome, which he undertook, though he was shipwrecked in the Adriatic on the way there. The immediate object of his mission was successful, through the good offices of Alityrus, a Jewish actor and a favourite of Nero, and Poppaea, the Emperor's wife, who was favourably inclined towards Judaism. The priests were released, and Josephus returned to Jerusalem, laden with gifts from Poppaea, and much impressed with what he had seen and heard of the Roman Empire.

The revolt which was to culminate in the destruction of Jerusalem was just beginning when he returned from his mission to Rome. To remain neutral in such a struggle was almost impossible. Open revolt was dangerous, however

---

[1] *B.J.* II. 119–67.   [2] *Life* 11.

[3] Ibid. 12. As the text stands there is some confusion. It is hard to see how he could have spent the whole of his three years of trial with Banus alone, since he says (§11) that he passed through the three sects as well in that time. The difficulty would be removed by reading παρ' αὐτοῖς (i.e. the three sects and Banus) for παρ' αὐτῷ.

[4] Ibid. 13–16.

justified the rebels were in their grievances, and Josephus tried to restrain them by insisting[1] upon the greater experience of the Romans in war. After his recent visit to Rome, he could appreciate this, although he was no doubt not alone in his view, and he realized that in the end such a revolt was doomed to failure. But reason could not prevail in the circumstances, however much Josephus pleaded his view and pointed to the "Fortune" of the Roman Empire in evidence of it. To hold such a minority view at that time was dangerous in the extreme, and even if it were done from the highest motives of policy was liable to serious misinterpretation. After making his protest in vain against the madness[2] of the rebel leaders, he was forced to take refuge in the Temple.[3] Apparently the high-priests and the chief of the Pharisees,[4] who agreed with Josephus' policy, were equally impotent, and could only await the intervention of the procurator Cestius Gallus, hoping thereby for a speedy end to the rebellion.[5]

But the unexpected defeat of Cestius Gallus at Bethhoron disappointed any such hopes, and gave the rebels fresh confidence for the time being, until the effect of the energetic counter-measures of the Roman government began to be felt. Anti-semitism, moreover, was showing itself in murders throughout Syria,[6] and this made the problem for the Roman administration still more complex and serious. In the interval the Sanhedrin had to decide upon a plan of action. According to Josephus, the principal men of Jerusalem[7] met and sent him with two other priests on a special mission to Galilee.

The purpose of this mission is highly problematical, and a special section is reserved in this book for its fuller treatment. Josephus' own statements about it are contradictory. Its purpose, he affirms on the one hand, was to deceive the robbers[8] and to pacify them: on the other hand, he says that he went as commander to organize further resistance against

---

[1] Ibid. 17.   [2] Ibid. 19.   [3] Ibid. 20.
[4] Ibid. 21.   [5] Ibid. 23.   [6] Ibid. 25–7.
[7] Ibid. 28.   [8] Ibid. 29.

Rome.[1] Feeling was running high on both sides, and Josephus'
activities pleased neither. It is sufficient here to give the outline
of events, and to mention facts as he relates them. Whatever
precisely was the purpose of his visit, he encountered much
opposition in Galilee. Some success attended his mission in
Sepphoris.[2] Tiberias was divided into three rival parties,[3]
and there were even splits in the separate sects. There was
anarchy at Gischala,[4] and in John of Gischala he found a
bitter, life-long enemy, who with Justus of Tiberias alleged at
Jerusalem that he was aiming at a tyranny. Gamala remained
loyal to the Roman government.[5]

After investigating the state of affairs, Josephus sent back
his report to the Sanhedrin, and asked for orders. He was
invited to stay and "take care of Galilee".[6] It seems that his
companions were not very anxious to continue, and were
soon dismissed [7] and sent back to Jerusalem. Josephus was now
in his thirtieth year,[8] and events were approaching a climax.
Vespasian, in the spring of A.D. 67, advanced against the
rebels,[9] and on his approach Josephus took refuge in the fortress
at Jotapata, a step which was dictated by desperation, for he
could not hope to withstand a siege by the Roman troops.
The Roman general called it deliberately "entering a prison".[10]
The besieged were divided amongst themselves, and Josephus
narrowly escaped murder, but still the hopeless siege lasted
for forty-seven days. He gives a very full account of events,[11]
which nevertheless shows signs of rhetorical exaggeration.
There was a suicide pact among the besieged, and the man
who drew the fatal lot was slain. His detractors, noting the
fact that Josephus escaped that fate, ascribed his escape to a
manipulation of the lots. So he was taken prisoner, and when
brought before Vespasian predicted that he would shortly
become emperor. Perhaps this was no more than an intelligent

[1] *B.J.* II. 562–3.   [2] *Life* 30.   [3] Ibid. 32–42.
[4] Ibid. 43–5.   [5] Ibid. 46–61.   [6] Ibid. 62.
[7] Ibid. 77.   [8] Ibid. 80.
[9] For the subsequent details, the main source is the *B.J.*
[10] *B.J.* III. 144.   [11] *B.J.* III. 384.

reading of the trend of events, which fear for his life emboldened him to utter. In any case, the incident is recorded in Suetonius,[1] and Josephus' life was spared.

The year of the Four Emperors (68–69) followed, full of significance for the Roman Empire, and in July A.D. 69 Vespasian was proclaimed emperor by his own soldiers. Josephus' prophecy was fulfilled, and in recognition of this he was set free. Henceforth he accompanied his erstwhile captors, visiting Alexandria [2] with Vespasian, and seeing the capture of Jerusalem by Titus (A.D. 70). Many times he went around the walls, exhorting the besieged to surrender.[3] After the capture of the city he returned to Rome with Titus, having received in recognition of his services a piece of land outside Jerusalem,[4] and obtained the release of some of his friends.[5]

His enemies were too numerous to allow him to live in safety at Jerusalem any longer. Instead, he settled at Rome. His own wishes in this matter coincided with necessity, so that the change was not irksome to him. There he stayed for the rest of his life. He was awarded Roman citizenship and a pension,[6] and lived in special apartments granted to him, where he wrote the history of the Jewish war for his patrons. He was henceforth known as Flavius Josephus.

He lived to see many changes in Rome during the remaining thirty or so years of his life, surviving Vespasian, Titus, and perhaps Domitian. It is possible that these years too saw changes in Josephus' own outlook, particularly towards his fellow-countrymen. At least, we still possess the *Jewish Antiquities* and the *Contra Apionem* which he wrote. Again and again he was accused of being a traitor, so that even while he lived in comparative safety in Rome, he was not allowed to forget the past by others, even if his own conscience was at ease. On the occasion of the revolt of Cyrene (A.D. 73) the accusations turned out to his own advantage. A certain Jonathan said that he had given secret support to the rebels

---

[1] *Vesp.* 5.   [2] *Life* 415, *Contra Ap.* I. 48.   [3] E.g. *B.J.* II. 362.
[4] *Life* 422.   [5] Ibid. 419, 421.   [6] Ibid. 323.

at Cyrene, but Vespasian rejected the calumny, and in token of his faith in him, granted him another estate in Judaea.[1]

Yet his anxieties increased after the death of Titus (A.D. 81), though he emerged triumphant. While Domitian's reign of terror caused Tacitus and Juvenal to cease their literary activities, Josephus received still further honours,[2] and his Jewish estates were exempted from taxes. During the "reign of terror", the *Jewish Antiquities* appeared, followed by the *Contra Apionem*, the title by which this defence of Judaism is generally known. He was preparing another work on the *Essence of God* and the *Laws of the Jews*,[3] but it was probably never finished, and certainly not published. His plan was perhaps interrupted by the incident which resulted in the work known as the *Life of Josephus*, which is not so much an autobiography, as an account of his career with special reference to that part of it which was criticized. His former antagonist, Justus of Tiberias, published a history of the Jewish War, in which Josephus was made out to be a traitor, a tyrant, and the cause of the outbreak of the war. Such a work needed refuting immediately, in view of the potential danger to Josephus' literary fame; moreover, in Domitian's principate, literary men were not very popular and had to be above suspicion. Josephus' answer is contained in the *Life*, which was added as an appendix to the *Antiquities*.

The exact date of his death is not known, but it may be assumed that he died at about the age of seventy. He was survived by three sons, Hyrcanus, born in A.D. 72, Justus, in A.D. 75, and Agrippa, in A.D. 77.[4] His married life does not seem to have been very happy, for he was married three times, first to a captive woman from Caesarea, after the siege of Jotapata. He soon divorced her, and married a woman from Alexandria,[5] while he was there with Vespasian. He had three children by her, but only Hyrcanus survived. Next he

---

[1] Ibid. 425.   [2] Ibid. 429.   [3] *Ant.* XX. 268.
[4] *Life* 5.   [5] Ibid. 415, 426 f.

married a Jewess from Crete, who was the mother of Justus
and Agrippa.

No memorial of him was set up in the city of his birth; it
was the city of his adoption which set up a statue in his
memory,[1] and put his works into the library at Rome. Jerusalem did not mourn his death, and even in Rome his name was
not long remembered or cherished.

Although Josephus was himself soon forgotten entirely, both
by his friends and his foes, his works remained. In this he is more
fortunate than some of the greatest authors of antiquity, whose
works have either perished with them completely, or are only
extant in tantalizingly small fragments. Posterity is thus in
a position to form some judgement about his works, and incidentally about the writer of them, and in this case particularly
so, inasmuch as his works contain a considerable number of
personal references by their writer.

The "Jewish War"

This is the first work of Josephus, written while he was in
Rome enjoying the benefits granted him by his patron, and is
his most famous. The prologue to it is important. He alleges
that the histories published hitherto of the War of the Jews
against the Romans culminating in the capture of Jerusalem
are unsatisfactory and inadequate: the historians, he maintains,
either took no active part themselves and have "gotten together vain and contradictory stories, and have written them
down in a sophistical style", or if they were eye-witnesses of
the events "have given false accounts of things, and this
either out of a humour of flattery to the Romans or of hatred
to the Jews"; moreover, he says "their writings contain
sometimes accusations, and sometimes encomiums, but no-
where the accurate truth of the facts".[2] In these circumstances,
Josephus decided "for the sake of such as live under the
government of the Romans, to translate those books into the

---

[1] Eus. *Hist. Eccl.* III. 9.   [2] *B.J.* I. 1.

2—S.I.J.

Greek tongue, which I formerly composed in the language of
our own country, and sent to the Upper Barbarians".[1]
Josephus' *Jewish War* was published in Greek about A.D. 75,[2]
the original in his own language Aramaic a year or so earlier.
Evidently little time was lost between the capture of Jerusalem and the end of the war before "histories" of it were
published, and it is therefore natural that these earliest
works suffered from the defects of their early publication,
because it takes some years before the necessary information in
such cases can be collected, digested, and used by an historian.
Josephus goes much further in his criticism: some of these
historians, he says "fail in their purpose . . . for they have a
mind to demonstrate the greatness of the Romans, while they
still diminish and lessen the actions of the Jews".[3] The Greek
historians, as he calls them, were likewise guilty of neglecting
the truth.[4] But, for himself, he claims that he was careful
not to go to the other extreme and become a biased supporter
of his own countrymen.[5] Such an intention is to be praised,
even if it is not admitted that he carried it out.

He goes on to state his conclusion, which he claims to
demonstrate in his history, that "they were the tyrants of the
Jews who brought the Roman power upon us, who unwillingly
attacked us, and occasioned the burning of our holy city".[6]
He promises that his accounts are given "without concealing
anything, or adding anything to the known truth of things",[7]
and ends with these words: "I have left no occasion for complaint or accusation to such as have been acquainted with this
war; and I have written it down for the sake of those that
love truth, but not for those that please themselves."[8] These
are bold claims, especially for a history in which such highly
controversial ideas are recorded, but they are impressive
and sound sincere. When compared with the introduction to

---

[1] *B.J.* I. 3. For the identification of these people see ibid. 6.
[2] Such is Whiston's computation.
[3] Ibid. 7.   [4] Ibid. 16.   [5] Ibid. 9.
[6] Ibid. 10.   [7] Ibid. 26.   [8] Ibid. 30.

Thucydides' *History of the Peloponnesian War*, the prologue to Josephus' *Jewish War* seems more high-sounding, but less confident. "My history", says Thucydides, "is an everlasting possession, not a prize composition which is heard and forgotten."[1] Yet we must bear in mind throughout what Dr Jowett said:[2] "It is commonplace . . . that we must interpret an ancient writer by himself, and by his own age, and not by our standards of right and wrong. . . . Nor can we argue from his inconsistencies or omission of details; nor draw inferences from his precise words, because we cannot expect him to use legal accuracy. The whole manner of ancient writing was different from our own."

Much depends, then, on Josephus' claim to truth. He writes in the same strain about his work in the *Contra Apionem*,[3] noting the prominent personages such as Vespasian and Titus who received, and those, such as Agrippa II, who bought copies: in the *Life* too [4] he mentions that "King Agrippa wrote sixty-two letters testifying to the truth of the record" and that Titus put his signature to the *Jewish War* and gave orders for its publication. Propaganda may have been one of the purposes for which it was composed, for it was the policy of the Roman emperors and also in their interests to preserve the peace of the Empire. We need not doubt the statement that it was among his intentions in writing "to comfort those that have been conquered by them, and to deter others from attempting innovations under their government"[5].

The actual title has received attention from commentators. Laqueur first pointed out [6] that the title refers to the war as the Romans would have referred to it: the Jews would have referred to the Roman War, most probably, or the War of the Jews against the Romans. The late Dr Thackeray [7] made much of this too, and connects it with the Slavonic Version, following

---

[1] Thuc. I. 22, trans. Jowett.   [2] Thuc. Vol. II, pp. xv, xvi.
[3] *Contra Ap.* I. 46 ff.   [4] *Life* 36 ff.   [5] *B.J.* III. 108.
[6] In *Der jüd. Historiker Fl. Josephus*, Giessen 1920.
[7] *Josephus the Man and the Historian*, New York 1929, pp. 29–34.

Dr Eisler. Such a theory is based on the title "Concerning the Capture (of Jerusalem)", found chiefly in one family of manuscripts, and claims that this was the earlier title used in the original Aramaic edition, and changed later when the work was published in Greek and made available to the Roman world.

It was not the purpose of Josephus in this work to preface his main theme with any long account of the earlier period of Jewish history, since others had already done this;[1] instead he decided to start with Antiochus Epiphanes (175–163 B.C.),[2] a point at which many had left off, and to devote the majority of his space to contemporary history.

The concluding words of his Preface [3] deserve to be quoted in full: "I have comprehended all these things in seven books: and have left no occasion for complaint or accusation to such as have been acquainted with this war: and I have written it down for the sake of those that love truth, but not for those that please themselves (with fictitious relations)."

We possess a synopsis of each book, from which the contents can be seen in a short and summarized version. The first book comprises the events from the reign of Antiochus Epiphanes to the death of Herod the Great (4 B.C.). The second book starts with the death of Herod the Great and ends with the mission of Vespasian to Palestine (A.D. 67); the third book goes on to the time of the taking of Gamala (A.D. 68); the fourth book ends with the coming of Titus to besiege Jerusalem (A.D. 69); the fifth book recounts the events of the first six months of the siege, and describes the straits to which the Jews were reduced; the sixth book goes as far as the capture of Jerusalem in A.D. 70; the seventh book describes the events of the next three years up to the revolt of Cyrene.

"And here", Josephus concludes,[4] "we shall put an end to this our history; wherein we formerly promised to deliver the same with all accuracy, to such as should be desirous of under-

[1] *B.J.* I. 17.
[2] Ibid. 19.
[3] Ibid. 30.
[4] *B.J.* VII. 454.

standing after what manner this war of the Romans with the Jews was managed. Of which history, how good the style is, must be left to the determination of the readers; but for the agreement with the facts, I shall not scruple to say, and that boldly, that truth hath been what I have alone aimed at through its entire composition."

This synopsis shows how Josephus planned his work and carried it out: the majority of the space is devoted to the immediate subject, namely the details of events leading up to the Fall of Jerusalem. His avowed purpose is made plain by constant and almost excessive reiteration.

THE "JEWISH ANTIQUITIES"

The next work of Josephus is the *Jewish Antiquities* in twenty books, his longest and most mature work. It took much longer to write, and bears signs of careful composition and sustained effort. Again, he writes a preface which, according to Whiston, "is excellent in its kind and highly worthy the repeated perusal of the reader, before he set about the perusal of the work itself". It should be added that the preface is also worth perusal after reading the work itself, so as to consider what he says in the main work in the light of his introductory claims and promises.

Josephus refers early in the Preface to the *Jewish War*, which he wrote because he was concerned with the facts and played a part personally in the events, and because he wished the public to have all the facts at their disposal in forming their conclusion.[1] But the *Antiquities* is not controversial in that sense. He promised to explain "who the Jews originally were":[2] this promise he is now fulfilling "as thinking it will appear to all the Greeks [3] worthy of their study". His debt to Epaphroditus is generously acknowledged, for he encouraged the author when his task seemed insuperable because of its size and the difficulty of writing fluently in a foreign tongue.[4] He warns his readers of the philosophy of history which

[1] *Ant.* I. 4–6. [2] Ibid. 6.
[3] I.e. the Gentiles, non-Jews. [4] Ibid. 7, 8.

underlies this work, that God was possessed of perfect virtue and that men also ought to strive after the participation of it, and that "on those who did not so think and so believe he inflicted the severest punishments".[1] "I exhort therefore my readers", he says,[2] "to examine this whole undertaking in that view."

He is therefore committed to a history of events from the earliest times, and starts with the Creation. The Old Testament is his main guide and source for the early books of the *Antiquities*. The contents of the books show the space which he devotes to events as they appear.

BOOK I.	From the Creation to the death of Isaac. (3,833 years.)[3]
BOOK II.	From the death of Isaac to the Exodus. (220 years.)
BOOK III.	From the Exodus to the rejection of that generation at Sinai. (2 years.)
BOOK IV.	From the rejection to the death of Moses. (38 years.)
BOOK V.	From the death of Moses to the death of Eli. (476 years.)
BOOK VI.	From the death of Eli to the death of Saul. (32 years.)
BOOK VII.	From the death of Saul to the death of David. (40 years.)
BOOK VIII.	From the death of David to the death of Ahab. (163 years.)
BOOK IX.	From the death of Ahab to the captivity of the Ten Tribes. (157 years.)
BOOK X.	From the captivity of the Ten Tribes to the first year of Cyrus. (182½ years.)
BOOK XI.	From the first year of Cyrus to the death of Alexander the Great. (253 years.)

[1] Ibid. 23, cf. 14.   [2] Ibid. 24.
[3] The figures in each case are those given by Whiston.

The *Antiquities* therefore contains "what hath been delivered
down to us from the original creation of man, until the twelfth
year of the reign of Nero", and gives the history of the Jews
in Egypt, Syria, and Palestine, besides their relations with
foreign powers in Palestine and the list of their high-priests
and Kings.[1]

In the first ten books the Biblical narrative is followed
closely, but in the last half of the work, which discusses events
after the Exile, the narrative is not so well proportioned. The
four hundred years which elapsed after the Exile to the death
of Judas Maccabaeus are compressed into Books X, XI, and

[1] *Ant.* XX. 258–61.

XII, but after that the author goes into more detail. The reign of Herod the Great covers three whole books (XIV–XVI) and is much fuller than the summary which is given in the *Jewish War*. Some discrepancies in the two accounts may be noted, and in general the account [1] in the *Antiquities* is more outspoken and critical of Herod. When he comes to the time of the Roman procurators also (A.D. 6) his account is detailed, and an account is given of each procuratorship. This work ends with Florus, the last of the procurators, and Josephus then refers his readers to the *Jewish War*, after the statement that it was "Florus who necessitated us to take up arms against the Romans, while we thought it better to be destroyed at once, than little by little".[2] There follow his final remarks, which include the now familiar claim about the accuracy of his narrative: "And I am so bold as to say, now I have so completely perfected the work I proposed to myself to do, that no other person, whether he were a Jew or foreigner, had he ever so great an inclination to it, could so accurately deliver these accounts to the Greeks as is done in these books."[3]

The "Life"

It was not the original intention of Josephus to append the *Life* to his *Antiquities*, and indeed, it looks as though we have a final paragraph added later by the writer to introduce this work. Circumstances accounted for his decision to write the *Life*, which is not so much an autobiography in the ordinary sense as a detailed apologia of his conduct in Galilee prior to the capture of Jerusalem in A.D. 70, intended to rebut the accusations made against his character and integrity. "And now", he says,[4] "it will not be perhaps an invidious thing if I treat briefly of my own family, and of the actions of my own life, while there are still living such as can either prove what I say to be false, or can attest that it is true." The work is

---

[1] E.g. *Ant.* XVI. 150 ff.   [2] *Ant.* XX. 257–8.
[3] Ibid. 262.   [4] *Ant.* XX. 267–8.

THE "CONTRA APIONEM"   15

indispensable for any full account of the life and career of
Josephus, and reference has already been made to it.[1]

It was his intention to publish the *Antiquities* and the *Life*
together, and his intention was fulfilled. They are dedicated to
the same patron, Epaphroditus, and the final sentence of the
Life is significant. "And this", he concludes,[2] "is the account
of my whole life: and let others judge of my character by them
as they please: but to thee, O Epaphroditus, thou most
excellent of men, do I dedicate all this treatise of our
Antiquities."

The "Contra Apionem"

If the *Life* of Josephus was added to the *Antiquities* chiefly in
self-defence against those who attacked his character, the
Contra Apionem was written chiefly in reply to those who
attacked his literary work, in particular the *Antiquities*. It is
comparatively short, containing two books, and was dedicated
to Epaphroditus.[3] If this is the same man to whom the *Antiquities* was dedicated,[4] we are provided with a rough date for its
composition. The *Antiquities* was first published in A.D. 93
or 94, without the *Life*, while Domitian was still alive. His
death took place in A.D. 96, and Epaphroditus was, it seems,
condemned by him. So the *Contra Apionem* must have been
written at the latest in 94 or 95, while Epaphroditus and
Domitian were still alive.

The exact title which Josephus gave to the book is somewhat doubtful; the Josephus manuscripts give *Concerning the
Antiquity of the Jews, against Apion*, and Origen refers to it
simply as the work *Concerning the Antiquity of the Jews*. The
title of the work as we now have it grew most probably out of a
reference by Eusebius [5] to refutations of Apion the grammarian,

---

[1] See the previous section on Josephus' life.
[2] *Life* 430.   [3] *Contra Ap.* I. 1.
[4] Dr Hudson ad loc. thinks that the Epaphroditus of *Contra Ap.* must be
a freedman and procurator of Trajan, and so dates the work later.
[5] *Hist. Eccl.* III. 8. 2.

and for the sake of brevity was called *Against Apion*. The addition to the title of the words "to the Greeks" by Porphyry [1]
has not been retained, and may be somewhat misleading.

This work, Josephus' last extant composition, is in some
respects the most curious of them all. He is concerned to defend
the antiquity of his nation as set forth in the *Antiquities* against
those who doubted it. According to Josephus, the grounds of
their objection are that the Jews "are not so much as vouch-
safed a bare mention by the most famous historiographers
among the Grecians",[2] and his aim is not only to produce
witnesses for his view, whose reputation for truth is admitted
by the Greeks, but to give the reasons why not many of the
Greek historians have mentioned the Jews in their works.[3]

He immediately launches into his familiar theme of truth
and accuracy in history, so that we have further incidental
references to his previous works; and he takes the opportunity
in effect to protest against the view that the Greeks are the
sole responsible historians of antiquity, because their historical
literature is of relatively late date.[4] He quotes too, obviously
with relish, cases of disagreement between Greek historians,
and mentions that: "Thucydides himself is accused by some
as writing what is false, although he seems to have given
us the exactest history of the affairs of his own time."[5] So
he infers that their evidence is not adequate on all subjects,
and is moreover of a comparatively late date, lacking such
official records as those compiled by the Jewish High-priests,
Egyptians, Chaldaeans, and Phoenicians. That some Greek
historians mention the Jewish people, while others ignore
them, he ascribes to deliberate suppression of facts.

In the second book he proceeds more particularly with his
main purpose, and answers the calumnies of Apion against the
Jews. It is understandable that the work has come to be known
as the *Contra Apionem*. Apion was an Alexandrian scholar who
lived in the reign of Tiberius (A.D. 14–37), and some of his

[1] *De abstinentia* IV. 11.   [2] *Contra Ap.* I. 2.
[3] Ibid. 4, 5.   [4] Ibid. 6–14.   [5] Ibid. 18.

writings, tinged with a strong anti-semitic flavour, were widely circulated in Rome. It has indeed been suggested that Tacitus derived from Apion his passage [1] on the origin of the Jews. First, Josephus enumerates some of the statements of Apion, leading up to his attack on the Jewish religion as a cult of the ass, vitiated by animal sacrifices, and never producing great men demanding respect. He adds, very bitterly, that Apion's miserable death was a well-deserved punishment,[2] and proceeds to attack the religious beliefs of the Greeks, which were certainly varied, and sometimes gross. Contrasting them with the Mosaic Law, he produces a spirited defence of the Jewish religion, which is constructive, and a classic of its kind.

But the whole work is not on a very high level. It must have been written quickly, and resembles a pamphlet, with all the pamphleteer's lavish use of the *argumentum ad hominem*. At least, however, we leave the last of Josephus' works with a vivid picture of him as an apologist for his people, writing fearlessly in their defence and conceding nothing to their detractors.

[1] *Hist.* V, 2–10. Cf. *Flavius Josèphe, Contra Apion.* Th. Reinach, Paris 1930, p. xviii.
[2] *Contra Ap.* II. 143.

CHAPTER 2

JOSEPHUS' "JEWISH WAR"

EFERENCE was made in the last chapter to the *Jewish War*. The purpose of this chapter is to examine this work in greater detail, to investigate the problems which it arouses, and to consider and assess its value as history. It is clear at the outset that it deals with debatable ground, because Josephus himself took part personally in the affairs which he recounts; he was later attacked by Justus of Tiberias for the part which he played at that time, and wrote the *Life*, which was appended to the *Antiquities*, in self-justification and self-defence. When we realize further that during the siege of Jerusalem Josephus was on the side of the Romans, and frequently urged his countrymen to surrender, it is all the more to be expected that he would be the centre of a controversy in which the facts might easily be obscured in the heat of the argument.

The contents of the *Jewish War* will therefore be considered first: much light is thrown upon them by the preface,[1] by reference to which they will later be assessed.

Josephus first explains the circumstances which led to the composition of the *Jewish War*. Originally, he wrote "in the language of our own country"[2] an account of these proceedings, but, in view of the many unreliable accounts which had been published, decided to produce a history in Greek for the benefit of those living under the Roman government. The Aramaic account was written for the benefit of the "upper barbarians", that is, as he explains later,[3] the Parthians, the Babylonians, the most remote inhabitants of Arabia,

---

[1] See also below, section 1.
[2] *B.J.* I. 3, i.e. Aramaic.   [3] Ibid. 6.

his fellow countrymen beyond the Euphrates, and the inhabitants of Adiabene. The work was obviously meant to provide
information and warning, and must have been written very
soon after the capture of Jerusalem. But its appeal was limited
to those who knew the language, and Josephus wished to
produce an account in Greek which would be available for
the Greeks and Romans, or, as we may say, the Hellenistic
world of his day, especially because there existed many
varied and varying accounts of the war, which, according to
Josephus, erred either on the side of excessive partiality to the
Romans or of hatred to the Jews.[1] The truth, as Josephus
sees it, is not to be found simply in magnifying the exploits of
the Jews: accuracy will demand that he should recognize
merits and faults on both sides. Josephus' claims to have
sought truth and accuracy are repeated elsewhere.[2]

Further information about the *Jewish War* in Greek is
given in the *Life*, written about thirty years later, and appended
to the *Antiquities*. The *Jewish War*, he says,[3] was presented,
immediately after it was finished, to Agrippa and Titus; both
commended it, the former requesting that the remainder of
the work be sent to him, and the latter expressing the hope
that Josephus' work might become, as it were, the official
history of the war. The work is also referred to in the *Contra
Apionem*:[4] there Josephus emphasizes the part which he himself played in the events which he describes, of which he kept
record, and mentions that in the composition of the work
in Rome he employed assistants for the sake of the Greek.

Josephus gives a synopsis of the contents of the *Jewish War*,
which he divided into seven books:[5]

BOOK I. From the capture of Jerusalem by Antiochus
Epiphanes to the death of Herod the Great.
BOOK II. From the death of Herod to Vespasian's
appointment as commander against the Jews.

---

[1] Ibid. 2. [2] E.g. *Ant.* I, preface. [3] *Life* 361 ff.
[4] *Contra Ap.* I. 46 ff. [5] *B.J.* I. 30.

Book III.   From the appointment of Vespasian to the siege
            of Gamala.
Book IV.   From the capture of Gamala to the approach
            of Titus against Jersalem.
Book V.   The siege of Jerusalem.
Book VI.   The capture of Jerusalem.
Book VII.   From the capture of Jerusalem to the revolt of
            the Jews at Cyrene.

In the final paragraph, he returns to the theme of the preface:
"And here we shall put an end to this our history; wherein
we formerly promised to deliver the same with all accuracy.
... Of which history, how good the style is, must be left to the
determination of the readers; but for the agreement with the
facts, I shall not scruple to say, and that boldly, that truth
hath been what I have alone aimed at through its entire
composition."[1]

The first book is of an introductory nature, giving an
historical resumé beginning at an important stage in Jewish
history; the second describes the revolt in Galilee and the
initial success of the Jews against the Romans at Bethhoron;
from the third to the sixth book we are presented with an
account of the chain of events culminating in the capture of
Jerusalem by Titus; in the seventh book, by way of epilogue
and perhaps of warning of the folly of resistance to the might
of the Roman Empire, is an account of the abortive revolt of
the Jews at Cyrene. There is no doubt that Josephus realized
the drama of the events which he described, and his narrative
is interwoven with sections which, while not inconsistent with
his theme, are of special interest and importance in themselves:
the picture drawn of the rise of the Herodian house;[2] the
Jewish sects, Pharisees, Sadducees, and Essenes;[3] the part
played by Josephus himself in Galilee,[4] and his rivalry with
John of Gischala;[5] the description of Galilee, Samaria, and

[1] *B.J.* VII. 454–5, trans. Whiston.   [2] *B.J.* I and II.
[3] *B.J.* II. 119–66, cf. *Ant.* XVIII. 11–25.   [4] *B.J.* II. 568ff.
[5] *B.J.* II. 585 ff.

Judea;[1] a description [2] of the Roman armies and their camps;[3] the siege of Jotapata and the capture of its garrison and commander Josephus by Vespasian;[4] the description of the river Jordan and the lake of Gennesareth;[5] the long account of John of Gischala;[6] the description of Jericho;[7] the description of Jerusalem, and of the Temple.[8] There is no doubt, judging from these passages that Josephus wrote as an eye-witness, and, moreover, as a person of some real knowledge of his theme. It is clear, too, that he sensed the disaster which befell Jerusalem at its capture, and appreciated, to an extent, its historical importance.

Our consideration of the *Jewish War* may conveniently be made under the following headings:

1. The circumstances in which it was written.
2. The sources with the aid of which it was composed.
3. The methods used in its composition.
4. The narrative as a trustworthy and credible document.

1. THE CIRCUMSTANCES IN WHICH THE "JEWISH WAR" WAS WRITTEN

Josephus himself throws light on this aspect of his work, and a closer examination of the relevant passages is now necessary. In the preface he mentions, with regret, the inadequacy of similar works on the same subject, some of which were composed by men who took no part in the events which they described, while others, written by men who took part, were coloured either by excessive partisanship towards the Romans or hatred towards the Jews.[9] His own intention, therefore, is to provide for those who live under the Roman government, an account translated into Greek of these events which originally

---

[1] *B.J.* III. 35 ff.
[2] Josephus calls it a "digression" in effect: *B.J.* III. 108-9.
[3] *B.J.* III. 70-107.   [4] *B.J.* III. 132-338.   [5] *B.J.* III. 506-21.
[6] *B.J.* IV. 389 ff.   [7] *B.J.* IV. 452-84.   [8] *B.J.* V. 184-247.
[9] I. 1-2.

were written in Aramaic for the benefit of the "Upper Barbarians";[1] he was by birth a Jew, a priest, who had himself
fought against the Romans and had been present at subsequent events of necessity,[2] and therefore, by implication, was
well qualified to give an accurate account of these events.
Truth and accuracy are a recurrent theme of Josephus,[3] and
he points out that his zeal for both led him to discern the faults
of Romans and Jews alike, because of his special relationship
with both sides. It can be expected therefore that what he
says may be controversial.

Further allusions to the composition of the *Jewish War* are
to be found in later works. In the *Life* [4] he declares that he
presented his work to the "Emperors themselves",[5] almost
in the course of the events themselves, and received testimony
for his accuracy; he also presented his work [6] to "many
others", some of whom had taken part in the war, such as
King Agrippa and certain of his relatives.[7] Titus put his own
signature to the work, and ordered its publication; Agrippa
wrote "sixty-two letters testifying to the truth of the narrative".[8] Josephus quotes two of them: the first [9] declares that
Josephus seems to have taken more pains over the details
than previous writers on that subject, and requests that the
other volumes be sent to him; the second [10] says that Josephus
"appears to stand in no need of instruction to enable us all to
learn from the beginning [*sc.*, of the war]. But when you meet
me, I myself also will acquaint you with many of the facts
not known." Agrippa evidently did not write to Josephus in
words of absolutely unqualified admiration; by indicating,
moreover, that there were facts not known, he implies that

---

[1] I.e. living in the upper Tigris region, near Parthia.
[2] I. 3.   [3] Cf. *Ant.* XX. 262.   [4] *Life* 361.
[5] This statement is somewhat vague: certainly Titus and Vespasian are
meant.
[6] *Life* 362.
[7] Except for the mention of King Agrippa and his relatives, this statement "to many others" is again too vague.
[8] *Life* 364.   [9] Ibid. 365.   [10] Ibid. 366.

Josephus himself did not know them. This may have affected the narrative to some extent. The other reference to the composition of the *Jewish War* is to be found in the *Contra Apionem*, where Josephus again insists on his veracity through having taken part in and witnessed the proceedings which he describes.[1] He adds [2] that he sold copies to many of the Romans who had fought (in the war) with him, and to many of his countrymen including Julius Archelaus, "the most venerable Herod",[3] and King Agrippa himself; all testified to his careful championship of the truth.

From all these allusions, it is clear that the *Jewish War* as we have it is a Greek edition of an earlier work in Aramaic, and that it received Roman commendation and became in a sense the official history of the war. It may not validly be concluded that because it was in a measure official it was partial, although it can be understood that this would be sufficient cause to discredit it in the eyes of some extremists. It may be noted that in the *Life* [4] Josephus says that he presented Agrippa with a copy, while in the *Contra Apionem* he says that he sold [5] it to him: such a discrepancy is comparatively insignificant.

With regard to the earlier Aramaic edition, as could be expected, there have been attempts to identify it from the Greek, although the Aramaic version as such is not extant. A clue is thought to be found in the fact that there are variants in the title of the work as it has come down to us. The usual title of the work is "Concerning the Jewish War". Josephus speaks of it as "the Jewish War",[6] or "the books written concerning the Jewish War".[7] The adjective "Jewish" as applied to the war means "against the Jews". This has been pointed out, especially by Laqueur.[8] Admittedly, the phrase is the one by which Romans would have referred to the war, whereas the Jews might have referred to it as the "Roman" war, but it means that Josephus, writing in Greek for Romans,

---

[1] *Contra Ap.* I. 47 ff.   [2] Ibid. 51.   [3] Not easily identified.
[4] 362.   [5] I. 51.   [6] *Ant.* I. 203; XVIII. 11.
[7] *Ant.* XX. 258, *Life* 412.   [8] Op. cit.

3—S.I.J.

used the title with which they were familiar. We cannot argue
further than that and conclude that the work is shown by its
title to be a worthless piece of Roman propaganda. But in
addition to the usual title, there are the variants. The Paris
manuscript (P) to which Niese assigns much authority, has
for the title, "Flavius Josephus' History of the Jewish War
against the Romans." Niese adopts this title in his edition.
Other manuscripts read "the Jewish history of Flavius
Josephus the Jew concerning the Capture", or something
essentially the same; the Latin version has "the histories of
Josephus"; Naber adopts the title "Concerning the Jewish
War, or the Jewish History concerning the Capture". It is
virtually impossible from the evidence to say what exactly
Josephus himself wrote as the title of his work, and it is clear
that there is no unanimity. From references elsewhere in
Josephus, it would appear that the "Jewish War" was sufficient for him; this title was expanded by the addition of
"against the Romans".[1] But the expanded title soon needed
radical curtailment, and "Concerning the Capture" (*sc.* of
Jerusalem) was used. This is to be found in Origen and Jerome,
the latter of whom ascribes the title to Josephus himself,
although, as Niese says, this is not so.[2] So there are two main
titles, "Concerning the Jewish War" with variants, and
"Concerning the Capture". A sufficient explanation of their
origin is to be sought in the manuscript tradition, on the lines
which we have just indicated. Dr Eisler,[3] however, has
elaborated the theory that the "Capture" was the title of the
original Aramaic draft, and that the "Jewish War" was the
title of the later Greek version. His theory stands or falls on
his identification of the "Capture" with the Aramaic version.
Dr Thackeray admitted [4] that he had been "gradually drawn

[1] Thus confusing the meaning of "Jewish", i.e. "against the Jews",
in the short title.
[2] "Ipsi tamen Josepho nullo modo tribuendus est", vol. VI, Praefatio,
p. iii.
[3] *The Messiah Jesus and John the Baptist*, Methuen, 1929.
[4] *Josephus*, p. 31.

to the theory of my old friend Dr Robert Eisler". If the theory is correct, it is most extraordinary and strange that no mention of the title the "Capture" as such appears in Josephus: the word ἅλωσις occurs in connection with the capture of Jerusalem, admittedly,[1] but it indicates very little, and certainly does not support Dr Eisler's theory, which in any case does not offer any real indication of the nature of the original Aramaic version.

It has been mentioned above that the *Jewish War* received Roman commendation, and became in a sense the official history of the war. At this point, therefore, we may consider this aspect of the work more fully, and examine the grounds on which it is based. It would be unfair to take the view that Vespasian, Titus, and Agrippa commended Josephus' work simply because it happened to appeal to them: the effective considerations must lie deeper than that. Among these considerations must have been the fact that Josephus himself was a Jew who had taken part in the war: his repeated claim to have been an eye-witness of the events which he related is not without significance. Moreover, Josephus [2] indicates that for at least part of the cause of the war between the Jews and the Romans the Jews themselves were responsible, a view which would wield greater weight with the Romans because it was held by a Jew. Indeed, there is much to be said in favour of the semi-official history of that war being written by a Jew if possible, because the narrative demanded reference to Jerusalem, the Temple, and the religion of the Jews, none of which was likely to appeal very strongly to the ordinary Roman. This whole matter is not to be considered simply as the case of a renegade Jew writing to curry favour with his present patrons and former enemies, because that view does scant justice to both the Romans and Josephus, and is too superficial. Again, is the work mere propaganda? This question is relevant here because of the modern tendency to equate all propaganda with the perversion or suppression of truth: it is

[1] *B.J.* II. 454; IV. 318; V. 3.　　　　[2] E.g. *B.J.* V. 442 ff.

important because of the implication that a work which is
propaganda is as such intrinsically untrustworthy. Wilhelm
Weber [1] maintained that the *Jewish War* is based on a "Flavian
work", which sought to extol the Flavian dynasty. The
Flavian work itself, he thought, opened with the account of
the disposition of the Roman legions, proceeded to the account
of the siege and capture of Jerusalem, and ended with the
triumph in Rome; Josephus simply expanded this account
with the first two and the last books of his *Jewish War*. This
theory is interesting not only because of its attempt to identify
the source which Josephus used in the *Jewish War*, but also
because of its interpretation of the value of the work as a
result of its propagandist aim. It must be admitted that the
work is from one point of view propagandist because it ex-
presses a policy and a conclusion which it seeks to substantiate
and spread; in general, this may be summarized negatively,
by saying that resistance to Roman arms was futile and bound
to be unsuccessful in the long run, and positively, that the
Roman Government worked on the whole beneficially for its
subjects. Opposition to the Romans lay much deeper, however, and was intimately concerned with the religion of the
Jews; nevertheless Josephus was evidently one of those who
did not find an irreconcilable conflict of loyalties between his
relationship with the Roman authorities and his obligations
to his nation and his God.

2. The sources with the aid of which the "Jewish War"
was composed

There is a great contrast between the *Jewish Antiquities* and
the *Jewish War*, in that the former mentions the sources of
information frequently, the latter hardly at all. In considering
the sources of the *Jewish War* we are therefore forced back
again to the prologue of the work, where emphasis is laid
on the importance of eye-witnesses of the events to ensure the
reliability of a narrative. The implication of this is that Jose-

[1] *Josephus und Vespasian*, Berlin 1921.

phus himself as an eye-witness of the events described in the *Jewish War* was therefore trustworthy, not needing to rely on information at second-hand. In justification of this he writes:[1] "But then, an undertaking to preserve the memory of what hath not been before recorded, and to represent the affairs of one's own time to those that come afterwards, is really worthy of praise and commendation. Now he is to be esteemed to have taken good pains in earnest, not who does no more than change the disposition and order of other men's works, but he who not only relates what had not been related before, but composes an entire body of history of his own."

The main source therefore of the *Jewish War* is Josephus' memory of what he saw and of the events in which he took part. This memory may well have been assisted, as he says,[2] by notes which he kept throughout the siege of Jerusalem of events in the Roman camp; information brought by deserters is also mentioned, presumably to indicate that his record was not completely one-sided. It is, of course, difficult for one person taking part in events such as these to know all that was going on, and see them all as a whole. Such a difficulty confronts war correspondents especially. But in the comparatively limited action of the siege of Jerusalem, we cannot deny that Josephus, by his position in the Roman camp alone, had sufficient material for composing that part of his work which recounts the siege: what went on inside the city was told him by deserters.

So far, this explanation of the main source of events during the siege of Jerusalem seems quite adequate, and there appears to be no need to deny Josephus' memory (and notes) as the *main* source for this period of the war. Yet, Thackeray's statement does not agree with this explanation: he says that [3] "apart from the early Galilaean campaign . . . his own notes and recollections are a comparatively minor factor in the narrative. The bulk of it appears to be derived from the documentary source of Roman origin." This is, in effect, the

[1] *B.J.* I. 15.   [2] *Contra Ap.* I. 46 ff.   [3] *Op. cit.* p. 37.

view of Wilhelm Weber,[1] which maintains that the narrative
of the *Jewish War* is based on a "Flavian Work", which traced
the rise of the Flavian dynasty, with particular emphasis upon
"Friedens-programm, Felicitas publica, und Vespasian der
Retter". According to Weber it is possible to detect the contents of this source which Josephus is thought to have followed
carefully and closely: the first two books of the *Jewish War*
introduce the "Flavian Work" which begins with the description of the disposition of the Roman legions and ends with
Rome's victory. Nevertheless, Thackeray dismisses this
particular theory on the grounds simply of the objection
"that the scathing reference which Josephus makes to previous
publications on the war renders it highly improbable that he
has based his narrative on a literary work of this nature".
Therefore, the "documentary source of Roman origin", which
Thackeray agrees in one place Josephus used, is not accepted
later when he rejects Weber's view, which in effect incorporates
this hypothesis. In fact, the very inconsistencies and difficulties
encountered when trying to uphold a view of a "documentary
source of Roman origin" behind the *Jewish War* seem, in
themselves, to provide evidence against it.

Thackeray then propounds the view[2] that Josephus had
access to the "commentaries" of Vespasian and Titus.[3] It
is strange that in the *Jewish War* the written source, if any,
is unnamed, whereas in the *Antiquities* such sources are often
named. There may have been a change of policy as a result of
Josephus' experience as a writer; or it may be that Josephus
had no consistent policy in this matter, in spite of the assump-
tions of modern writers about him that he was so consistent.
At their face value Josephus' statements state and imply that
for the *Jewish War* his own memory and notes formed the
main source, in which case his silence about any subsidiary
source can be explained and understood: where there is a

---

[1] *Josephus und Vespasian*, Berlin 1921, esp. pp. 58–88.
[2] Ibid. p. 38.
[3] Referred to in *Life* 342, 358; *Contra Ap.* I. 56.

main source, as for example in the *Antiquities*, he mentions it. The references to the disposition of the Roman legions in A.D. 66 are important and, in part, apparently confirmed by excavations.[1] We may reasonably infer that such precise information came from a Roman source with which Josephus was able to check his narrative. Beyond this it seems unnecessary to go, lest hypotheses be multiplied and confusion arise.

3. The methods used in the composition of the "Jewish War"

In view of Josephus' statement that he made use of assistants for the Greek version of his *Jewish War*, their work needs to be considered mainly in this section. Is it possible to identify these assistants and the sections for which they were responsible? Or is there no evidence that they were given a certain section to write, but rather acted as revisers of Josephus' Greek? The whole matter concerns indirectly the theory of the Sophoclean and Thucydidean assistants in the *Antiquities*, because if the work of the assistants in the *Jewish War* can be identified, it may provide at least an analogy and perhaps a basis for considering the theory of their assistance in the *Antiquities*; but if their work in the *Jewish War* cannot be identified, where they were admittedly used, it may be difficult also to identify their work in the *Antiquities*, where their presence is purely hypothetical. A consideration of the speeches in the *Jewish War* will also be shown to be relevant to this consideration of the work of the assistants and of the methods of composition used.

The names and social status of the assistants are, as Thackeray said,[2] unrecorded, and he hazarded the guess that they were Josephus' slaves. He also admitted [3] that he had not "so far succeeded in discriminating the respective contributions of the two or more members of his literary staff

---

[1] J. M. Allegro: *The Dead Sea Scrolls* (Pelican Books 1956), p. 86.
[2] Op. cit. p. 105.   [3] Op. cit. p. 106.

employed on the War". This investigation into the nature of the work of the assistants in the *Jewish War* is therefore bound to be mainly linguistic.

Starting with a comparison of the *Jewish War* and the *Antiquities*, it is noticeable that many constructions and words are common to both.

(i) The absence of connecting particles is very frequent, and indeed can be said to be characteristic. As a result of his use of asyndeton the idiomatic connecting γάρ is omitted, and a form of τοιοῦτος or οὗτος used alone.[1] Connecting particles are nevertheless used,[2] but even so his use of them is sometimes cumbersome.[3]

(ii) The perfect and pluperfect tenses are found where an aorist would have been more idiomatic, and the participles are not always neatly constructed and subordinated to the main verb.

(iii) Abstract expressions are noteworthy, especially ἐπί with the dative of an abstract noun to express purpose, and ποιεῖσθαι with the accusative of an abstract noun to express the equivalent of the corresponding verb.

(iv) A curious form of involution occurs, whereby the words are put in a most unusual and awkward order, for no apparent reason.[4]

These characteristics are to be found in both works, and though not in themselves conclusive evidence either way, yet they help if anything to support the thesis of a common authorship of the *Antiquities* and the *Jewish War*, as distinct from that of separate assistants responsible for the composition of the latter work.

The language and vocabulary of these two works now need investigation, because if considerable similarities and

---

[1] E.g. τοιοῦτος *Ant.* XV. 18, XVI. 328: οὗτος XI. 215, etc.

[2] E.g. XX. 113.

[3] E.g. the odd use of τοιγαροῦν, second word, XIII. 44, 130.

[4] Cf. *Life* 338: Ἰοῦστος γοῦν συγγράφειν τὰς περὶ τοῦτον ἐπιχειρήσας πράξεις τὸν πόλεμον: B.J. I. 242 τεθεραπευκὼς οὐκ ὀλίγοις Ἀντώνιον χρήμασιν.

parallels can be indicated, they too will provide some cumu-
lative evidence. For example, ἀπόγνωσις (=ἀπόγνοια) is
found in the *Jewish War* and in the *Antiquities*; likewise,
ἐρεθίζω, the phrase πρόνοια θεοῦ, ἠρεμέω, δραστήριος, εὐπραγία,
κακοπραγία, αὔτανδρος, προκόπτω (intransitive), σπάνις (-ίζω),
προσέχω (without τὸν νοῦν), ἰλυσπάομαι, ῥαΐζω, δασμός, ἀμέλει.
There is therefore some indication that the language and
vocabulary of these two works have something in common;
bearing in mind the rather special character of some of the
words, it can hardly be said that the phenomenon is merely
accidental. It is especially noteworthy that in the last book of
the *Jewish War*, the style and vocabulary contain no words,
phrases, or constructions which could not have come from
Josephus' own pen: the book, as regards style and vocabularly,
is exactly like the last book of the *Antiquities*, without any
appreciable difference. Thackeray suggested [1] that towards
the end of the *Jewish War* Josephus was thrown "more and
more upon his own resources", after the experience gained
by the use of his "assistant" in the earlier books. This may
be the case, but the characteristics common to the *Jewish War*
and the *Antiquities*, examples of which were noted above,
militate against the implication, which is the basis of
Thackeray's view, that earlier books of the *Jewish War* show
the unmistakable signs of composition by the "assistant".
The fact becomes more and more plain, upon closer investigation, that in the *Jewish War* the admitted assistance received
by Josephus was not in the form either of a revision by the
assistants of Josephus' amateurish drafts, or of their own
writing purely and simply; it is highly improbable that a
particular assistant wrote specific sections of the *Jewish War*
for Josephus, because there is an underlying unity in the
work which must be adequately accounted for, as well as
the apparent differences between the *Jewish War* and the
Antiquities.

These apparent differences consist largely of a certain type

[1] Op. cit., p. 105.

of word peculiar to the *Jewish War*. The list of such words given by Thackeray[1] includes the following:

ἀδιάλειπτος, ἄτονος, διεκπαίειν, διέχειν (= ἀπέχειν elsewhere in Josephus), εἰκαῖος, ἐξαπίνης (rather than ἐξαίφνης), κοπιᾶν, λαθραῖος, λεωφόρος, μεσημβρινός, μεταγενέστερος, μόνον οὐκ (= μικροῦ [δεῖν] elsewhere), ὀλόφυρσις, ὀρρωδεῖν (and compounds), παλινδρομεῖν, πανοῦργος, παράστημα, πρὸς δέ (adv: = καὶ προσέτι elsewhere), πτοεῖσθαι, συνάφεια, διὰ τάχους, κατὰ τάχος, χθαμαλός, χωρισμός. Many of these words are semi-poetical or rare.[2]

To these words found alone in the *Jewish War* and not in Josephus' other works may be added poetical words such as: ἀναιμωτί, ἄρκυς (in the plural), ἀφειδέω, βῶλος, δέλεαρ, δυσίατος, ἔκυρά, κηλίς, κληδών, μειλίσσομαι, μεταίχμιος, ξυστόν, πελειάς, πρόρριζος, πτῶμα (corpse), σκέπτομαι, σταλαγμός, σμήκω, στιβαρός, τερέβινθος, τύφομαι, χερμάς, φρενοβλάβεια.

Thus the style of the *Jewish War* is in part elaborate and somewhat ornate, being coloured by such poetical words. It is therefore akin to the Atticistic style which became popular in the first century A.D., as a reaction against the artificial pedantry of the Alexandrian age, though it was more polished than the Hellenistic Greek. As a literary composition, the *Jewish War* is on the whole the most polished of Josephus' works.

Herein lies a clue to the work of the "assistants". It is, on the available evidence, impossible to identify with any certainty specific "assistants" for specific books or parts of books, such as the "Thucydidean" and "Sophoclean" assistants of Thackeray. Poetical and rare words are found throughout the work, so that it cannot be validly inferred that they are the product of an assistant's pen who was responsible for a part.

---

[1] *Lexicon*, Intro., Part I, p. viii: this list is almost identical with that given in the Loeb Josephus, vol. III, p. xiv.

[2] E.g. παράστημα in Diod. and Dio. Hal: παλινδρομέω in Diod. and Plut.

(i) Poetical and rare words found in each of six books of the *Jewish War*: ἠρεμέω, παράστημα, προσέχω (om. τὸν νοῦν).

(ii) in each of five books: ἀδόκητος, δραστήριος, δυσωπέω, κειμήλιον.

(iii) in each of four books: ἀγανάκτησις, ἀλιτήριος, αὔτανδρος, εὐπραγία, θερμός (metaphorical), νύσσω (= stab), πταῖσμα (and compounds), χερμάς.

(iv) in each of three books: ἀστοχέω, δυσθανατέω (-άω), ἐπικουφίζω, εὐτονέω, κακοπραγία, καραδοκέω, μειλίσσομαι (-ττ-), νεύματι (νεῦμα), παλινδρομέω, πειθήνιος, φοινικών, φρενοβλάβεια.

(v) in each of two books: ἀδήριτος, ἀκαταιτίατος, ἀναιμωτί, ἀναρροιζέω, ἀρειμάνιος, γείσιον, δέλεαρ, διανυκτερεύω, διαπρύσιος, διωρία, εὐθηνία, λυττάω, ναστός, νήφω, ὀλιγότης, πειθαρχέω, πολιά, πολυάνδριον, προαγνεύω, προσανέχω, πτῶμα (= corpse), σοβαρός, ὑποκόπτω, φιλοψυχέω, φιμόω, χειροκοπέω.

There is thus evidence for a connecting link between all these books, and in view of the poetical and rare words which form this evidence it can reasonably be interpreted as indicating a unity of authorship in the main, that is, Josephus himself.

What then exactly was the nature of the work of the "assistants" in the *Jewish War*? Briefly, to polish and improve Josephus' completed "translation" of the work from the original Aramaic. This would account for the impression of polish which is predominant in the *Jewish War*. Whether the presence of such embellishment in the form of vivid, highly coloured words and phrases is in fact an improvement may be open to debate. The following words and phrases are most significant in this connection, and may with some confidence be assigned to the assistants:

(i) πρίν with the genitive: πρὶν ἀνηκέστου πάθους I. 121, II. 233, 320, VI. 123: πρὶν τῆς εὐχῆς II. 131: πρὶν ἀνηκέστου συμφορᾶς V. 372. This usage is not found in the *Antiquities* and is not characteristic of Josephus himself. Similarly, δι' ὄχλου εἶναι (of that which is hackneyed) in II. 251, IV. 496.

(ii) the concessive use of καίπερ and καίτοι. καίπερ I. 437, 581; III. 137; IV. 18, 410; V. 15; VI. 24, 385. καίτοι I. 249, 349, 530, 579, 606; II. 372, 385, 617; IV. 25, 317; V. 446; VI. 5, 356, 383. No instance of either usage occurs in the last book. That the two words should appear fairly consistently throughout the work is significant, but when they appear very close together (καίπερ I. 581; IV. 18; VI. 385: καίτοι I. 579; IV. 25; VI. 382), it is of especial significance. καίτοι is used in the same sense in *Ant.* XIV. 430, 480; XVI. 242, and in *Ant.* XV. 119 καίπερ is used in the same sense. καίτοι therefore appears to be the word which Josephus himself wrote; the assistants changed it to καίπερ, but were not thorough in their change.

(iii) the use of κειμήλιον fourteen times in the *Jewish War* suggests that the assistants were fond of it. It also occurs in *Ant.* XIV. 410; XV. 6, but these examples are not so strained as the one which occurs in *B.J.* III. 408.

(iv) variations in the forms 'Εσσηνός and 'Εσσαῖος. The normal form is 'Εσσηνός and can be said to be characteristic of Josephus.[1] For the sake of embellishment and polishing, the assistants seem to have used the form 'Εσσαῖος. The two forms occur close together in II. 113 and 119, and as with καίπερ and καίτοι[2] must indicate two hands at work. The form 'Εσσαῖος in *Ant.* XVII 346 is at first sight puzzling, but Josephus is here using the *Jewish War* as his source,[3] and may be said to have imported the form 'Εσσαῖος. The occurrence of 'Εσσαῖοι in *Ant.* XV. 371, so close to 'Εσσηνῶν (XV. 373) is likewise puzzling, but the Latin version of the former is *esseni*, and may suggest that 'Εσσηνοί was the form in some manuscripts, so that the confusion may be due in this case to manuscript tradition rather than to Josephus himself.

(v) ἀξινάριον II. 137 and ἀξινίδιον II. 149 provide similar

---

[1] *B.J.* II. 119. *Ant.* XIII. 171, 172, 311; XV 373; XVIII. 18.
[2] Cf. (ii) supra.
[3] *Ant.* XVII. 346 describes the same event as *B.J.* II. 113 which has Εσσαῖος.

evidence of more than one hand, though in this case it is difficult to know which should be ascribed to Josephus.

The evidence adduced confirms that Josephus, as he himself says, used assistants "for the sake of the Greek", but suggests that their task was to improve and embellish the diction of Josephus' completed Greek draft of the *Jewish War* which he had translated from the Aramaic. It can be said with some emphasis on the evidence shown that Josephus did not hand over to the assistants and make them entirely responsible for any particular part of the work. The presence of Josephus can be detected throughout, and the amount of work done by the assistants is not as great as might be supposed. In fact, as a result of this consideration, the work done by Josephus needs to be emphasized rather than the work of his assistants.

4. THE NARRATIVE AS A TRUSTWORTHY AND CREDIBLE DOCU-
MENT, WITH SPECIAL REFERENCE TO JOSEPHUS' MISSION IN
GALILEE

The three previous sections should leave us in a position to estimate the value and trustworthiness of the *Jewish War* as a record of events. There is nothing to cause a prejudice against Josephus; indeed, the opposite is rather the case, especially in view of the last section which upholds the view that Josephus himself was responsible for the most important part of this work, leaving only comparatively minor details of embellishment to his assistants.

The fact that the work quite frankly extols the power of Rome and can therefore be said to be propagandist in its purpose, has raised doubts about its general trustworthiness, but already an attempt has been made to indicate that such doubts are not entirely justified.[1] Josephus wrote the truth as he saw it: the fact that in his view the power and fortune of the Roman Empire were of paramount importance does not in itself render his work untrustworthy, any more than a similar view held by Polybius rendered his work untrustworthy.

[1] See esp. section 1 above.

The answer to the trustworthiness or otherwise of Josephus in the *Jewish War* hinges upon the part which he himself took in that War, for which he was most violently attacked, as he himself admits.[1] The part which he played is described in some detail in the *Jewish War* and the *Life;* the two accounts reveal discrepancies which, according to Thackeray, are "unaccountable",[2] and deal with the six months in which he was in Galilee.

We have two facts which in themselves are not necessarily inconsistent, but which to many of Josephus' contemporaries were manifestly irreconcilable:

(i) In A.D. 63 he went to Rome on a mission on behalf of certain Jewish priests.

(ii) Soon afterwards, at the end of his stay in Galilee, he was fighting against the Romans, and was besieged by them for forty-seven days in the town of Jotapata, before being captured.

There is no doubt about these facts, but their explanation is not clear, inasmuch as a number of factors, personal and political alike, are involved. Nevertheless, in the light of these facts, discrepancies may be expected and indeed are to be found in the *Jewish War* and the *Life*. In order to attempt to arrive at the truth we must first consider these facts and the accounts of them in some detail.

The visit to Rome took place, as he says,[3] "after his twenty-sixth year",[4] i.e. in A.D. 63 or 64. Its purpose was to obtain the release of certain Jewish priests who had been sent to Rome by Felix during his procuratorship of Judaea.[5] The circumstances surrounding their dispatch to Rome "to give an account to Caesar" are not mentioned: the shipwreck of Josephus on the voyage to Rome is reminiscent of the shipwreck of St Paul, who himself had "appealed to Caesar". Josephus became friendly with Alityrus, a Jew and a favourite

---

[1] *B.J.* III. 436–9.   [2] Op. cit. p. 49.   [3] *Life* 13–16.
[4] Or, it may be translated, "after his twenty-sixth birthday".
[5] A.D. 52–60.

at the Imperial Court, who by his good offices with Poppaea, Nero's wife, assisted in the release of the prisoners. We do not know why the priests were imprisoned and sent to Rome for trial,[1] nor in what capacity Josephus was dispatched to plead for them; he simply calls them his "friends",[2] and mentions that in addition to their release he obtained "liberal gifts". Prejudice against Josephus can easily make much of this reference to gifts; they were either symbols of friendliness or means of bribery. In any case, as soon as he returned home Josephus records that he attempted to dissuade those who were meditating revolt from Rome,[3] on the grounds that they were inferior "in military experience and fortune". Josephus was evidently impressed with the grandeur of Rome, so that the futility of opposition to her power seemed clear to him. Subsequent events proved him right in this view. But another factor emerged, which Josephus candidly records: he was so afraid that he would be hated and suspected as pro-Roman that he took refuge in the Temple for a time, and then joined the "chief priests and the chief of the Pharisees". They were in a dilemma, but decided to pretend that they agreed with the revolutionaries, and to counsel restraint, hoping that Cestius Gallus would soon arrive and put an end to the revolt. This policy was weak, and in fact would have pleased neither the Romans nor the Jews who wanted to revolt: it depended for its success upon Cestius Gallus' speedy arrival with adequate forces to put down the trouble. But Gallus' defeat at Bethhoron was an unexpected victory for the Jews, and meant that the policy of Josephus and his friends had failed.

What was to be their new policy? After Bethhoron their dilemma was even more complicated. According to Josephus,[4] the rebels were well provided with arms, and the authorities at Jerusalem were afraid that they would gain control by force; moreover the whole of Galilee had not yet revolted

---

[1] With the parallel with St Paul in mind it might be conjectured that they were Roman citizens, but that would be mere conjecture.
[2] συνήθεις ἐμοί, ibid. 13.   [3] Ibid. 17 ff.   [4] Ibid. 28 ff.

from the Romans. Therefore he, with two other priests Joazar and Judas,[1] was sent on a mission to Galilee, the purpose of which was not so much to pacify that territory, as to curb the more headstrong of the rebels; such a purpose could easily be misrepresented, for indeed we have to consider carefully what Josephus says about it to avoid misunderstanding. Apparently, the policy which he was sent to support was to wait and see what action the Romans would take, and by this means to quieten some of the violent opposition. Considered as a policy, it can be easily and forcefully criticized if only on the ground that it advocated surrendering to the Romans the initiative which the Jews had wrested from them at Beth-horon. In the *Jewish War*, however,[2] Josephus is portrayed as an officially appointed general for the conduct of the war against Rome; his command was Galilee with the addition of Gamala.

Of these two apparently contradictory accounts, that in the *Life* purports to be fuller because in that work Josephus claims to give facts "passed over until now",[3] relating to his work in Galilee for which Justus of Tiberias had violently attacked him. He immediately adds a significant statement to the effect that no surprise should be felt that he did not reveal these facts hitherto (i.e. in the *Jewish War*), because although it is the historian's duty to tell the truth, "it is permissible for him nevertheless not to accuse bitterly the wickedness of certain people, not because of favour towards them but because of his own moderation". In fact, Josephus admits that he did not give a full picture of this episode in the *Jewish War*, and claims to do so in the *Life*. It is unfortunate that he justified such suppression of facts on the grounds of laudable self-restraint.

In the *Jewish War* Josephus says that he went to Galilee at the outset in command of the rebels there; the *Life* says

---

[1] They are called καλοὺς κἀγαθούς, which is the term applied to the priests whose release Josephus negotiated.
[2] *B.J.* II. 562–8.   [3] 338–9.

that he went there to advocate restraint and later took part in the rebellion. Galilee was overrun with powerful bands of "robbers" who were violently anti-Roman [1] and opposed to any policy of restraint whatsoever. Here again we meet differing accounts given of John of Gischala, Josephus' opponent. In the *Jewish War* John is depicted [2] as crafty, treacherous, and deceitful, without apparently a redeeming feature: in the *Life* the picture is fuller [3] because it describes how John tried to restrain the elation in Gischala at the revolt from the Romans. In retaliation, the extremists destroyed Gischala, but John attacked again, gained possession of Gischala, and rebuilt it much more strongly than before.

Josephus' mission was not successful. "I saw that it was not in my power to disarm the robbers."[4] He therefore persuaded the people to pay them, for he wanted peace before anything else in Galilee. His colleagues left for Jerusalem, presumably thinking that since their mission was unsuccessful they ought to report for further instructions. They may also have objected to Josephus' policy of paying the "robbers" sums of money on the grounds that it was a confession of defeat and a surrender to blackmail. A new decision about this mission and future policy in Galilee was now clearly necessary. Incidents had occurred which had aroused suspicion: Josephus had kept the corn in Upper Galilee "either", as he says,[5] "for the Romans or for my own use", on the assumption that he had been put in command; and when there were spoils from the raid on the baggage of the wife of Ptolemaeus, steward of Agrippa, Josephus did not immediately divide them with the "robbers" who claimed a share.[6] John of Gischala therefore sent a request to Jerusalem for the removal of Josephus. A party of four was sent to supersede Josephus, but he outwitted them. The authorities at Jerusalem had by now clearly decided that the original plan of restraint was no longer possible.

---

[1] *Sicarii*: they may have some connection with the "Zealots".
[2] II. 585 ff.   [3] 43 ff.   [4] 77 ff.
[5] 72.   [6] 126 ff. cf. *B.J.* II. 595 ff.

4—S.I.J.

So in order to keep his position as "general" in view of this development in policy, Josephus was forced to show his hand as anti-Roman, which hitherto he had not wished to do. His position as "general" was more or less assumed, and was by now technically *ultra vires*. This would account for the different versions in the *Jewish War* and the *Life*, though of course he did not fail to assert in the *Life*, in a passage directed against Justus of Tiberias, that he was appointed general by the community of Jerusalem,[1] and that the appointment was properly regularized.[2] His first skirmish with the Roman forces is described in a manner consistent with this view;[3] he says that he kept his forces together "pretending to get ready to fight with Placidus", and records the consternation [4] of the Roman commander. Soon afterwards some of his followers deserted him, perhaps in protest at his change of attitude.[5]

All this intricate manœuvre and intrigue the account in the *Jewish War* has omitted, simply stating that Josephus was a "general" from the beginning. Such a statement is not completely true and Josephus must stand convicted to an extent of *suppressio veri*. He would no doubt have pleaded in his favour that this statement was sufficient for the Romans under whose auspices the book was written.

After this the position of Josephus in Galilee was not in dispute. He was soon besieged in Jotapata and captured, but he was well treated and was active throughout the rest of the war, especially at the siege of Jerusalem, in urging capitulation to the Roman forces.

The account of Josephus' mission in Galilee as given in the *Jewish War* is therefore incomplete. His actions caused much

---

[1] 341.   [2] 310.   [3] 213 ff.

[4] $\kappa\alpha\tau\alpha\pi\lambda\eta\tau\tau\acute{o}\mu\epsilon\nu\sigma$, cf. *Ant.* IV. 9: Whiston, "he was afraid". So Hudson, *prae metu*. The word means panic-stricken, or astounded, but not necessarily through fear. In this case, Josephus' change of attitude would account for the consternation.

[5] *B.J.* III. 129 f.

controversy and hostility in his lifetime, and it is still difficult to assess the facts with certainty because we cannot precisely judge his motives. That he was aiming at a "tyranny" as John of Gischala alleged is an over-statement; that he is guilty of inconsistency and in a measure of suppressing some of the facts in the *Jewish War* must be admitted. Those who were responsible in Jerusalem for the conduct of the war must also bear a share of blame because they underestimated the power and influence of the "robbers", especially in Galilee. Josephus must be acquitted of the charge of premeditated treachery.

Is the *Jewish War* then a trustworthy document? On the whole, the answer must be in the affirmative, in spite of the limitation indicated by the foregoing consideration of Josephus' mission in Galilee, which is, after all, only a comparatively small incident in the whole series of events which led up to the capture of Jerusalem in A.D. 70. It must be borne in mind that it is a work written with a purpose, and from a certain point of view; but in assessing its value, even if we disagree with its purpose and underlying point of view that the power of Rome was irresistible, we have a work which cannot justly be ignored, and which would even repay closer attention than sometimes it receives. Similarly, the view taken of the character of the author must not be allowed to create a prejudice against his work.

CHAPTER 3

JOSEPHUS AS A JEWISH APOLOGIST

The *Contra Apionem*

"IT may be fairly inferred", wrote Professor Moore,[1] "that Josephus, like most of the aristocratic priesthood to which he belonged, had little interest in religion for its own sake, and that his natural antipathy to all excess of zeal was deepened by the catastrophe which religious fanatics had brought upon his people." This statement might be interpreted as meaning that Josephus did not possess sufficient interest to write on the subject of religion: such an interpretation would not be borne out by the facts. At the end of the *Jewish Antiquities*, Josephus mentioned his intention to write "three books concerning our Jewish opinions about God and his essence, and about our laws; why, according to them, some things are permitted us to do, and others are prohibited".[2]

It would appear that Josephus did not write this book, for we have no evidence of its existence nor any reference to it. We possess the work known as the *Contra Apionem*. Whether this is the originally planned work, slightly altered in scope, we have now no means of determining precisely; on the whole, perhaps it is not. Probably the original intention was never carried out, but only something on the same sort of general lines. The attacks of the opponents of Judaism may have stung Josephus into writing the *Contra Apionem* instead of the projected work.

---

[1] *Judaism*, I. 210. [2] *Ant.* XX. 268, Whiston's translation.

The *Contra Apionem* was composed after the *Antiquities*,[1] to which reference is made, and was dedicated, like the *Antiquities*, to Epaphroditus, the patron of Josephus and publisher of his works. It was the last major work of Josephus. The *Life* alludes to the death of Agrippa II,[2] and was therefore written after A.D. 100. Epaphroditus is presumed to have died in A.D. 96,[3] so that the *Contra Apionem* can be supposed to have been written between that date and the first publication of the *Antiquities* in A.D. 94.

The title of the work is not that originally given to it by Josephus; it appears for the first time in Jerome.[4] It is convenient, because Apion is one of the opponents of Judaism who is referred to in the work; it might be misleading, if allowed to give the impression that the work is something in the nature of a mere pamphlet, the purpose of which is more destructive of the opponent's case than constructive in the presentation of Judaism. Earlier titles by which the work was referred to are, *Against the Gentiles*,[5] and *Concerning the Antiquity of the Jews*.[6]

The contents of the work are the best guide to the author's purpose and treatment of his theme. It is divided into two books, the first of which is concerned with the question of the antiquity of the Jews. This is precisely the sort of question which may have arisen when the *Antiquities* was published, so that Josephus takes an opportunity in the *Contra Apionem*[7] to consider it at length. He promises[8] to cite authors considered trustworthy by the Greeks, and to show why few Greek historians mentioned the Jewish people in their histories. His general thesis at this stage is that the Greeks are untrustworthy on matters of antiquity because they themselves are of comparatively recent origin. The oldest Greek writing is Homer, which

---

[1] *Contra Ap.* I. 1, 54; II. 287.   [2] A.D. 100, Photius.

[3] He is supposed to have been killed in the Domitianic persecution A.D. 96. (*Flavius Josèphe Contra Apion*. T. Reinach, Paris 1930. Introduction, p. xv.)

[4] Epist. 70, c. 3.   [5] Porphyry, *De abstinentia* 4, 11.
[6] Origen and Eusebius.   [7] I. 3.   [8] I. 4, 5.

was clearly composed after the Trojan war.[1] (It is note-worthy
that this reference to Homer and oral tradition was vital to
Wolf's *Prolegomena*, which opened up a new chapter in
Homeric criticism and study.) The Greek historians contradict
themselves, and even Thucydides is accused of error.[2] This is
due principally to lack of official accounts, Josephus alleges,
and also to lack of concern for truth among their historians.[3]
By contrast, the Jews took pains to compile official accounts,
and showed a great concern for truth. This leads Josephus to
speak of the Old Testament, the five books of Moses, the
thirteen books of the prophets, and four containing hymns to
God and moral precepts for man.[4] A digression on the *Jewish
War* follows, in which he declares again his concern for truth
and accuracy, not only in that work, but also in the *Antiquities*.[5]

Apparently great stress was laid on the allegation that the
Greek historians did not mention the Jews, in support of the
argument that the Jews were not an ancient people:[6] Josephus
declares his purpose of rebutting that allegation, and of
producing evidence from writers of other nations in contra-
diction of it. His plan is now clear.

The Greek historians, he says, did not mention the Jews because they did not know them, not because they did not then
exist.[7] Of the non-Greek historians who testify to the existence
(and antiquity) of the Jews he quotes Manetho,[8] the Phoeni-
cian annals, and Dios [9] the historian of Phoenicia and Menan-
der of Ephesus, the Chaldaean annals and Berosus the
Chaldaean historian.[10] References to the Jews do, however,
exist in the Greek historians, Pythagoras of Samos, Herodotus,
Choerilus, Clearobus, Hecataeus, Agatharchides,[11] and others.

How did these calumnies arise? Originally, Josephus
asserts, from the Egyptians,[12] who hated the Jews. As an
example of this attitude, he first quotes Manetho again,[13]

[1] I. 12.   [2] I. 15–18.   [3] 24.
[4] 39, 40.   [5] 47–56.   [6] 58.
[7] 60–8.   [8] 73 ff.   [9] 106 ff.
[10] 128 ff.   [11] 161 ff.   [12] 223 ff.
[13] 228 ff.

and criticizes his statements at length;[1] next Chaeremon,[2] and Lysimachus.[3] After criticizing their statements too, he breaks off, since his book has already reached a suitable length.[4]

The second book opens with a brief resumé of the first, and proceeds straightway to further consideration of "the authors who wrote against us". Here the grammarian Apion [5] is mentioned for the first time, but Josephus refutes his allegations at greater length; for example, the statement that the Jews were of Egyptian origin.[6] There were, apparently, similar accusations against the Jews in Alexandria which Josephus rebuts. A new note is now struck in this work, for after mentioning the esteem in which some of the kings of Egypt held the Jews, he states that the Emperor Augustus acknowledged their services.[7] Apion's calumnies are next rebutted that the Jews worship the head of an ass,[8] and practise ritual murder,[9] and such like.[10] There the treatment of Apion ends, and Josephus proceeds to refute the errors of Apollonius Molon and Lysimachus,[11] declaring that, compared with Moses, men like Lycurgus and Solon and Zaleucus are only recent. This leads him to an appreciation of the Jewish law-giver, with comments on the Jewish way of life under the influence of the Mosaic law and its theocratic constitution. Examples follow,[12] which are intended clearly to inform his readers as well as to illustrate his thesis, and then the religion of the Greeks is compared and contrasted with that of the Jews.[13] After a brief resumé of the whole work, it ends with a final dedication to Epaphroditus, and to all those who through his efforts may wish to know about the Jewish race.

There is no doubt that in this work Josephus feels strongly and shows his sentiments fearlessly and resolutely: his exposure of some of the accusations brought against the Jews and his

[1] 251–87. [2] 288 ff. [3] 304 ff.
[4] 320. [5] II. 2. [6] 28 ff.
[7] 61. [8] 79 ff. [9] 89 ff.
[10] Up to 144. [11] 145 ff. [12] E.g. 199 ff.
[13] 236 ff.

vigorous counter-attack leave no doubt of his fearlessness, while his exposition of the meaning of the Law shows conviction and resolution. In evidence of the latter, one passage is especially noteworthy. Speaking of Judaism he writes: "What form of government then can be more holy than this? What more worthy kind of worship can be paid to God than we pay, where the entire body of the people are prepared for religion, where an extraordinary degree of care is required in the priests, and where the whole polity is so ordered as if it were a certain religious solemnity? . . . All men ought to follow this Being, and to worship him in the exercise of virtue; for this way of worship of God is the most holy of all others."[1]

This is a fine piece of writing, and shows Josephus at his best. Perhaps he would have wished to be remembered as an apologist for Judaism first and foremost. In the Law he found an "everlasting possession"; Thucydides hoped that his history of the Peloponnesian War would merit that title. Therein lies a fundamental and ultimate difference of outlook, which is most significant.

Having now briefly considered the *Contra Apionem*, with special reference to its contents, we are in a position to examine some of the major problems raised in that work:

1. The nature of the opposition to Judaism as illustrated in the *Contra Apionem*.
2. The nature of the exposition of Judaism.

Anti-semitism existed in the first century A.D., and was sometimes manifested in dangerous forms: at the same time there existed the Jewish apologetic, which was designed to counter anti-semitism. It would be a mistake to magnify these two contending forces, and to compress all the problems of those days under that one issue, but it cannot be ignored as irrelevant or insignificant. The consideration of these

[1] *Contra Ap.* II. 188 ff.

problems will raise questions of particular methods used by the individuals mentioned in the *Contra Apionem*, including Josephus himself.

1. THE OPPOSITION TO JUDAISM IN THE "CONTRA APIONEM"

The *Contra Apionem* is of special value for its treatment of the literary opposition to Judaism, and the references made to the opponents illustrate the nature of the opposition not only in the first century A.D., but from about the second century before Christ.

(*a*) Manetho [1] wrote an Egyptian history in Greek, between 270 and 250 B.C.,[2] "translated from the sacred tablets". Josephus has two long references to this work, the first of which includes a lengthy quotation [3] from the second book of his history of Egypt, about the Hyksos. This quotation is impressive for its detail. The second reference [4] is of a different kind, because there Manetho admits that he is narrating current legends concerning the Jews,[5] which Josephus has no difficulty in demonstrating to be false. Bearing in mind the fact that Manetho states that he is only narrating popular tales concerning the Jews, one may wonder why Josephus goes to such length in disproving them, while attacking Manetho himself violently. Presumably such tales died hard, and formed part of the anti-semitic propaganda of Josephus' day.[6] The question has been raised of the authenticity of the quotations. Reinach declared [7] that it was of small importance whether the first quotation was first or second-hand; the second reference has been thought to be a later insertion, but in the absence of any considerable portions of Manetho large

---

[1] *Contra Ap.* I. 73–105, 228–87 (or Manethos).
[2] In the time of Ptolemy II Philadelphus.
[3] Ibid. 73–105; quotation 75–82.
[4] Ibid. 228–87.   [5] *Contra Ap.* I. 229.
[6] Whiston ad loc. seeks to explain why "our usually cool and candid author, Josephus . . . was betrayed into a greater heat and passion than ordinary".
[7] *Contra Ap.* I. 74, note 3.

enough to permit an assessment to be carefully made, such a hypothesis seems very laboured and hardly justified.

(*b*) Apollonius Molon is mentioned several times as an opponent of Judaism. "Moreover, since this Apollonius does not do like Apion, and lay a continued accusation against us, but does it only by starts, and up and down his discourse, while he sometimes reproaches us as atheists, and man-haters, and sometimes hits us in the teeth with our want of courage, and yet sometimes, on the contrary, accuses us of too great boldness, and madness in our conduct. . . ."[1] No quotations or exact references are given from this author, and, to judge from Josephus' statements about him, it would seem that his attacks on the Jews were particularly ill-informed.

Sometimes he is referred to as Apollonius Molon,[2] sometimes as Molon,[3] sometimes as Apollonius.[4] He was a teacher of rhetoric, born at Alabanda in Caria, who afterwards lived at Rhodes. Cicero as a young man first heard the lectures of an Apollonius Molon at Rhodes in 87 B.C., and continued as his pupil nine years later.[5] This tutor of Cicero was often known as Molon, and is to be distinguished from the other Apollonius Molon to whom Josephus refers. The Apollonius mentioned by Josephus was older than his name-sake and fellow-countryman; he was teaching in Rhodes when Scaevola went there as praetor in 121 B.C.[6] His work was an attack on the Jews, including allegations against Moses and the Law.[7] Josephus, in reply, decided to show that the Jewish laws contained very often ordinances quite different from the allegations of Apollonius, and in turn heaped upon Apollonius accusations of foolishness and blindness.[8]

(*c*) Lysimachus is referred to by Josephus as an opponent of the Jews. Little is known of him, and he may be identical

---

[1] Ibid. II. 148 (Whiston's translation).
[2] E.g. *Contra Ap.* II. 79, 145, 255.
[3] E.g. II. 16, 236.   [4] E.g. II. 148, 262.
[5] G. C. Richards, *Cicero*. London 1935, p. 14.
[6] Cic. *De Oratore* 1. 17, 75.
[7] *Contra Ap.* II. 145.   [8] Ibid. 255 ff.

with the Lysimachus who wrote Θηβαϊκὰ παράδοξα and
Νόστοι (i.e. of Greek heroes from Troy).[1] Perhaps he was an
Egyptian. His accusations seem absurd, e.g. that the Jews were
lepers,[2] and that they were expelled under Bocchoris, king of
Egypt, their leader being Moses. Josephus does not give the
exact quotation from Lysimachus, but uses *oratio obliqua*. The
date of the Exodus, and Lysimachus' reference to it, is mentioned again[3] later, and Lysimachus is coupled with Apollonius
Molon "and certain others" as a writer of "unjust and
untrue" statements about Moses and the laws.[4] Judging from
Josephus his history was not of a high standard, and it was
not difficult to rebut his statements.

(*d*) Chaeremon[5] is mentioned once only. According to
Josephus, he wrote a history of Egypt, which is quoted, as in
the case of Lysimachus, in *oratio obliqua*. It seems that the
work of Chaeremon was similar, in tone and outlook, to that
of Manetho. Porphyry refers[6] to the work of Chaeremon the
Stoic: this is apparently the same person. The fact that he is
called a Stoic is interesting, especially as he was an Egyptian
priest himself. He may also be the Chaeremon who was tutor
to the Emperor Nero. His work would represent the anti-
semitic views held in Josephus' own day, especially in an
important centre such as Alexandria.

(*e*) Apion's attacks upon Judaism were singled out for special
treatment;[7] hence the title now ascribed to this work of
Josephus. Apion the grammarian was born in Egypt, came to
Alexandria, and became famous as a grammarian. Suidas
states[8] that he taught in Rome in the time of Tiberius and
Claudius, and delivered lectures in Greece during the
principate of Gaius. According to Josephus,[9] Apion visited
Rome under Gaius as spokesman of the Alexandrians against
the Jews. There is no doubt of his hostility to the Jews.

---

[1] Schürer, *Jewish People*, div. 2, vol. 3, p. 254.
[2] *Contra Ap.* I. 305. [3] II. 16.
[4] II. 145. [5] I. 288–303.
[6] *De abstinentia* 4. 6–8. [7] *Contra Ap.* II. 2–144.
[8] *Lex.* v.s. Ἀπίων. [9] Ant. XVIII. 257 ff.

Pliny [1] says that "Apion wrote that those to whom he dedicated a composition had his gift of immortality bestowed upon them". If that is true, how absurd! And, moreover, how vain! Pliny in the same passage also says, in a revealing parenthesis, that Tiberius called Apion the "world's cymbal",[2] i.e. "as making the world ring with his ostentatious disputations".[3] Josephus' statement [4] that Apion congratulated Alexandria on having such a citizen as himself is consistent with such a character.

He wrote much, and gained a considerable reputation for his work on Homer, but Josephus was only concerned with his *History of Egypt*, of which he mentions specifically the third book,[5] and gives a quotation. It is hardly necessary to suppose [6] that he wrote a book entitled *Against the Jews*, for that is an inference from the *Contra Apionem* of Josephus, which, incidentally, mentions no such work, but only the *History of Egypt*. This inference was first drawn by Clement of Alexandria.[7]

According to Josephus, the grounds of Apion's attack on the Jews were threefold:

   (i) The departure of the Jews from Egypt.
  (ii) That the Alexandrine Jews disturbed the peace.
 (iii) The Jewish laws and worship.

So he refutes these accusations one by one.[8] It seems that Apion's attack was connected with a deep-seated enmity for the Jews, to whom he appears willing to give no credit whatsoever. Josephus in turn attacked Apion without mercy, and saw a fitting and ironical retribution for his blasphemies in the fact that he died in terrible agony, having been circumcised in an attempt to save his life. "This", he says, "was the end of

---

[1] *Hist. Nat.* praef. 25.   [2] *Cymbalum mundi.*
[3] Lewis and Short, Latin Dictionary, v.s. *cymbalum*, II.
[4] *Contra Ap.* II. 135.   [5] II. 10 f.
[6] As in art. "Apion", Smith & Wace, *Dict. of Christian Biography.*
[7] Schürer, op. cit., 2. 3. 259, discusses the matter in full.
[8] (i) in *Contra Ap.* II. 12–32; (ii) 33 ff; (iii) 79 ff.

Apion's life, and this shall be the conclusion of our discourse about him."[1]

These writers, to whom Josephus refers in detail, afford an opportunity to assess the nature of the opposition to Judaism. It appears to have been trivial and superficial, perpetuating similar if not identical accusations (e.g., about the Jews' worship of the head of an ass); it was focused upon the origin of the Jewish people, and upon the allegation, with variations, that they were expelled from Egypt as undesirable (e.g., the accusations that they were cast out because they were lepers). Such calumnies could be refuted without much difficulty, but the picture of anti-semitism which Josephus paints in the *Contra Apionem* contains an additional important element, which brought it up to date: this was the accusation that the Jews, by virtue of their religion, were anti-social, and more concerned in the affairs of the "clan" than in the interests of the community in which they lived.[2] (This factor is significant, because if accepted as an explanation of the Jewish way of life, it justifies suspicion of them as citizens, and creates readiness to make them scapegoats as trouble-makers.)

Especially in the case of Apion, all this prejudice against the Jews is seen as a contemporary problem, not simply as something past and gone. This problem was most urgent in Alexandria where Apion lived, and, no doubt, was accepted as an exponent of these anti-semitic views. In Alexandria, the situation was complicated by the privileged position of the Jews who were given a status equivalent to that of "Macedonians".[3]

Feelings against the Jews in the Greek cities began to run high and find expression in the middle of the second century B.C.

[1] 144.
[2] Josephus throughout the *Contra Ap.* seems to refer primarily to the Jews of the Dispersion, rather than to the Palestinian Jews: anti-semitism would be felt more directly by the former, and as such probably would be more familiar to Josephus.
[3] *Contra Ap.* II. 36, see *Cambridge Ancient History*, vol. IX, p. 431, note 1, but the reference there given is *Contra Ap.* II. 37.

Alexander the Great seems to have favoured the Jews, such being his policy in general; but when the implications of the Hellenism which he brought to his conquered lands began to be seen, and conquered peoples were encouraged to take part in Greek festivities and practices aimed at binding them all together in the brotherhood of Greek culture, some of the Jews at least began to dissociate themselves. Hence they were suspect, and became the butt of attacks, culminating in the pogroms at Alexandria beginning in A.D. 38.[1] Up to that time, the attacks were chiefly on paper, but the atmosphere was hostile; it would not be too much to say that this long-standing enmity was connected with the events which led to the revolt of Judaea and the capture of Jerusalem.

It was not a hostility for which a well reasoned and logical case could be made out, but rather that on both sides feelings were allowed to run high, and as time went on the hostility was inherited and the process became less and less logical. Josephus is right in speaking much more of the hostility which Apion and other writers nursed against the Jews, rather than of any one particular cause of the quarrel. Feelings ran high on both sides, and the more scurrilous the allegation which gave vent to these feelings, the more currency it received. This would explain why in the writers mentioned by Josephus the accusations against the Jews and the opposition to Judaism are similar.

In this connection, it cannot be ignored that the Jews seem, unfortunately, in spite of all their virtues and their great contribution to mankind, to possess the aptitude of arousing antagonism, consciously and unconsciously. This trait, which is so difficult to diagnose and account for, runs through all their history. In a sense, anti-semitism, throughout Jewish history, follows the same general pattern.[2]

[1] *C.A.H.* IX, p. 433, and X, p. 310.
[2] Cf. H. Belloc, *The Jews, passim*.

2. The exposition of Judaism in the "Contra Apionem"

It could be expected that if the Jews were attacked, they would answer, and *vice versa*. This very human characteristic accounts for the particular angle from which a considerable portion of Jewish literature in the Hellenistic age was written, so that we can expect to see this apologetic element present in the literature of Hellenistic Judaism, even if the particular work was not written expressly for the "Greeks" who had no concern with Judaism. A good example in this connection is the "Wisdom of Solomon",[1] of which, speaking generally, it could be said that we have here the truths of Judaism affirmed and expressed in the poetical and philosophical terms which would be familiar to Greeks.

Much therefore depended on these attempts to expound Judaism to non-Jews in terms with which they were familiar;[2] on them ultimately depended the hope of bridging the gap between Hellenism and Judaism. There was a clash between them under Antiochus Epiphanes,[3] as a result of which Hellenism was violently repudiated by the Jews because of its connection with pagan religion, and Judaism was violently repudiated by the Hellenists as narrow and anti-social.

Against this historical background, the apology of Josephus must be considered. We cannot fail to note the violence of his feelings and the personalities involved, especially in regard to Apion, so that there is in a sense some repetition. More positively, he claims that the Jews can stand comparison with any other nation as regards their antiquity, origin, culture, and religion. Perhaps Josephus paid special attention to this last subject because he was a Pharisee and a Jewish priest; it was specially important in view of the accusation that the Jews were contemptuous of the gods.[4] He expounds in effect

[1] Dated c. 100 B.C. *New Commentary*, S.P.C.K., Apocrypha, p. 70.
[2] In this connection the work of Philo is important.
[3] 175–163 B.C.
[4] By Apollonius Molon and Posidonius, *Contra Ap.* II. 79; cf. Pliny *H.N.* XIII. 4, 46; Tac. *Hist.* V. 5, *contemnere deos.*

the advantages, spiritually and philosophically, of monotheism, contrasted with polytheism. The same charge of contempt for the gods leads Josephus to answer the associated charge of Apion that the Jews refused to worship the Roman emperor,[1] and were therefore dangerous. He replies that a sacrifice was daily offered for the emperor in the Temple at Jerusalem.[2]

Through all this exposition there runs, like a thread, his respect for the Jewish Law, of which he writes in glowing terms. Here is a feature which he shares with Jewish apologists, but, even if the reader of the *Contra Apionem* agrees in general with Josephus in respecting the Jewish Law, there remains the difficulty of expounding satisfactorily the justification for such an attitude. For Josephus it is, on the whole, sufficient to say that such and such an observance is enjoined in the Jewish Law; no further need for its defence and support in his view exists, because the Law is for him the criterion. Logically, his attitude amounts to this: such and such an observance is enjoined in the Law, and therein lies its authority; if asked why the Law possesses that final authority, he would reply, because it is the Law, given to Moses for the Jews by God. That is sufficient and final. But for those like the Hellenists who did not accept a monotheism, nor even necessarily a theism in the strict sense of the word, this was unsatisfactory. And so the argument went on. Moreover, throughout his exposition of Judaism, there runs a view of the divine inspiration of the Jewish Scriptures.[3] One can imagine the Hellenists requiring further information about the manner of this divine inspiration, and the evidence for the Mosaic authorship of some of the books, but Josephus does not deal with any such matters. He was content to dilate on the Law, or to resort to a vigorous attack upon his opponents, which was one of the chief weapons of Jewish apologetics. In this respect also, Josephus is typical of Jewish apologists. But it did not help to bridge the gap be-

---

[1] *Contra Ap.* II. 73.   [2] Ibid. 77, cf. *B.J.* II. 194 ff.
[3] For an account of the Jewish Scriptures referred to in *Contra Ap.* by Josephus, see the Note appended to this chapter.

tween Judaism and Hellenism. The attitude and work of Philo were likely to make a contribution of greater value than that of Josephus towards this end, and in this sense Hellenistic Judaism held a key position. "When after the fall of Jerusalem Judaism all over the world became Hebrew and Rabbinic, Hellenistic Judaism, as such, withered away. The Synagogue casts its works upon the scrap-heap. . . ."[1]

That was the end of Jewish apologetics. Josephus' *Contra Apionem* is one of its most note-worthy productions, which does credit to its author and the cause on behalf of which he wrote.

NOTE

The Jewish Scriptures referred to by Josephus in the "Contra Apionem" (1. 37 ff.)

In contrast to the countless "divergent and contradictory" books of the non-Jews, Josephus claims with pride that the Jews have only "twenty-two books containing a record of all time and deservedly trusted":

(i) *Five* of these are the books of Moses, i.e. the Pentateuch (ibid. 39).
(ii) *Thirteen* prophetical books (ibid. 40).
(iii) *Four* containing hymns to God and moral precepts for men (ibid. 40). I.e., Psalms and Song of Songs; Proverbs and Ecclesiastes.

Thus, he arranged the Canon of Scripture into three parts, the law, the prophets, and the sacred writings, which he calls "hymns" because the Psalms were the first in this section. It is not quite the normal arrangement. His list contains a total of twenty-two books, whereas the Septuagint and the Talmud contain twenty-four.

It is clear, therefore, that this passage is important not only for the Canon with which Josephus himself was familiar, but it also raises further matters, such as Josephus' connection

---

[1] *C.A.H.* vol. IX. p. 436.
5—s.i.j.

with Palestinian or Alexandrian Judaism: the fixing of the Jewish Old Testament Canon was more or less contemporaneous with the *Contra Apionem*, i.e., the end of the first century A.D.

Origen and Jerome enumerate twenty-two books, which indicates that Josephus is not alone in his view, and that he did not accept the Septuagint number, which is twenty-four. The probable reason for this is that the twenty-two books were commonly accepted in the Palestinian tradition, in which Josephus was brought up, and from which also Origen and Jerome derived their information.

The five books of Moses, known as the Pentateuch, are easy to identify and present no difficulty (Genesis, Exodus, Leviticus, Numbers, Deuteronomy): the four "containing hymns" are generally agreed to be Psalms and Song of Songs, Proverbs and Ecclesiastes. The thirteen prophetical books cannot be identified with the same certainty. They are probably as follows:

1. Joshua
2. Judges and Ruth (counted as one book)
3. 1 and 2 Samuel (counted as one book)
4. 1 and 2 Kings (counted as one book)
5. 1 and 2 Chronicles (counted as one book)
6. Ezra and Nehemiah (counted as one book)
7. Esther
8. Isaiah
9. Jeremiah and Lamentations (counted as one book)
10. Ezekiel
11. Daniel
12. 12 minor prophets (counted as one book)
13. Job

The twenty-four books of the Septuagint and Talmudic Canon are not different from those in Josephus and the Palestinian Canon: the smaller number was reached by counting two sets of two books, probably Judges with Ruth, and Jeremiah with Lamentations as two instead of four.

This reference in Josephus to twenty-two books of the Jewish Scriptures is important also because it gives his views on the essential marks needful in such books:

1. They contain divine doctrines; hence their absolute authority.
2. Because they contain divine doctrines, they are deemed holy, and therefore are to be distinguished as comprising in themselves a special category.
3. Nothing has been added nor taken away from them because they belong to this special category; that is not permitted.
4. They must have been written within the period from the death of Moses to the reign of Artaxerxes, King of Persia.

1. The first of these essential marks of canonicity is propounded in the opening sentence of the passage referred to (*Contra Ap.* 1. 37) ... "we have only twenty-two books, which contain the record of all the past times, and which are rightly believed in". Eusebius, referring to this passage (*Hist. Eccl.* 3. 10) apparently added the work θεῖα (i.e. "believed to be divine"), which does not occur in the Greek or Latin texts of Josephus. Eusebius probably had in mind the statement of Josephus later in this passage, "it is become natural to all Jews ... to esteem these books to contain divine doctrines".

2. The view that these books are distinct is amplified in the description of the Scriptures as "the holy books" (in *B.J.*, *Ant.*, *Life*, and *Contra Ap.*). Hence, in the very use of the adjective "holy", which implies being set apart for a particular purpose, Josephus makes clear the distinctness of the category to which in his view the canonical scriptures belong.

3. "For during so many ages which have already passed, no one has been so bold as either to add anything to them, to take anything from them, or to make any change in them." Hence we have another characteristic of these books.

4. Josephus also states that all the canonical books were

written within a given period of time: the Pentateuch, belonging to Moses, contains the laws and the history of man from his origin until the death of Moses (traditionally about 3,000 years); from the death of Moses until the reign of Artaxerxes,[1] King of Persia, the prophets who came after Moses wrote in thirteen books (i.e. a period of about 600 or 700 years). Then follows a very significant statement: "But from Artaxerxes to our times all things have indeed been written down, but are not esteemed worthy of a like authority because the exact succession of the prophets was wanting." No book therefore which was not written within the period from Moses to Artaxerxes could qualify for canonicity. This is consistent with the official Jewish teaching, which ultimately found expression in the Talmud.

[1] 464–424 B.C. This would, in Josephus' view, argue for the canonicity of the Book of Esther, which mentions King Ahasuerus (or Artaxerxes).

CHAPTER 4

THE "JEWISH ANTIQUITIES"

with special reference to Josephus' "Assistants"

"I TURN to consider him in another aspect, as the Hellenist, trained in all the riches of Greek learning. But with him I would here associate others to whom he is immensely indebted. We hear much from our author of his own achievements: we hear little of those skilled and assiduous helpers in the background, who were no mere amanuenses, but polished his periods, occasionally took over the composition of large portions of the narrative, and hunted up, made extracts from, and translated into elegant Greek, edicts, acts, and other relevant records written in crabbed Latin characters and deposited in the imperial archives in the Roman Capitol. These anonymous menials deserve recognition for their invaluable services, and, in considering our author as Hellenist, instead of leaving him in solitary grandeur, we should do them justice by speaking of 'Josephus and Co.' "

This passage forms part of the opening paragraph of the fourth lecture by the late Dr Thackeray.[1] The picture is vividly painted, and, as the nature of the work performed by the assistants is elaborated in the course of the lecture, the work of Josephus himself thereby diminishes in extent and importance. The same view is taken in the incomplete Loeb edition of Josephus,[2] which was begun by Thackeray, and continued after his death by Dr Marcus.

The implications of this view are important, and deserve

---

[1] *Josephus the Man and the Historian*, H. St J. Thackeray, New York 1929, p. 100.

[2] Vol. 4, pp. xiv ff: see also *C.A.H.* X. 886.

reconsideration. We need to ascertain, for example, the precise grounds for the view and the evidence upon which it is based. In the passage just quoted, it is clear that the assistants are thought to have been given a very free hand as assistants, in "polishing his (Josephus') periods", and taking over occasionally "the composition of large portions of the narrative": they were responsible, in other words, for the final form in which the narrative was published. They are also described as "hunting up" relevant Latin documents in the Roman Imperial archives, and translating them into "elegant Greek": they were responsible, in other words, for the authorities consulted and quoted in the narrative.

There must surely be evidence in plenty for such a view, if the part played by Josephus in "Josephus and Co." is of such comparative insignificance. Josephus, in fact, makes only one explicit reference to "assistants", in the *Contra Apionem*,[1] when speaking of his first work the *Jewish War*: "afterward I got leisure at Rome; and when all my materials were prepared for that work, I made use of some persons to assist me in learning the Greek tongue, and by these means I composed the history of those transactions." The translation is inexact; the original χρησάμενός τισι πρὸς τὴν Ἑλληνίδα φωνὴν συνεργοῖς makes no mention of assistants for "learning" the Greek tongue; it says that he used assistants "for the Greek tongue", which is a much vaguer statement. It must be noted, moreover, that the mention of assistants refers only to the composition of the *Jewish War*, and only then as it were incidentally, for in the whole of that passage (47–52) he is defending the *truth* of his narrative in that work.

Thackeray ascribes to these "assistants" the good qualities which he detects in the *Jewish War*. "The style", he says,[2] "is an excellent specimen of the Atticistic Greek of the first century, modelled on, if not quite on a level with, that of the great masters of the age of Pericles"; he concludes that "these and other excellencies combine to give the work high

[1] I. 50, Whiston's translation.   [2] Op. cit., p. 104.

rank in Greek literature". There is no attempt to detect the respective contributions of the assistants in the *Jewish War*, where their work is admitted by Josephus: Thackeray, however, detects two of the assistants at work in the *Jewish Antiquities*, in which work Josephus makes no reference to assistants.

The detailed elaboration of this theory is important for its understanding and reconsideration. The writing of the *Jewish Antiquities* was contemplated by Josephus when he wrote the *Jewish War*;[1] he decided to finish the *Jewish War* and proceed separately with the other work. As time went on "there was hesitation and delay on my part in rendering so vast a subject into a foreign and unfamiliar tongue."[2] Is it possible to detect a point at which "hesitation and delay" took place? Thackeray suggested the end of *Ant.* XIV, the point at which Jerusalem was captured by Herod in 37 B.C. and "Herod came into the kingdom conferred on him three years earlier in Rome". Just before the end of *Ant.* XIV, an "indication of weariness"[3] could be detected: "after it begins a new manner of dealing with the author's materials, accompanied by a change of style." He therefore inferred that *Ant.* XV, XVI, XVII, XVIII, XIX. 1–275 (or 277) were the work of two assistants: the first two of these books being composed by the "Sophoclean", and the remainder by the "Thucydidean" assistant. The hypothesis was supported by analysis of the style, and the assistants were so described because of the similarity of their style to that of Sophocles and Thucydides respectively.

The theory is based on three main factors:

(i) Josephus' language difficulty.
(ii) Josephus' use of his sources.
(iii) The differences in style.

Thackeray supports his theory by a consideration of the

[1] *Ant.*. I. 6. [2] *Ant.* I. 7, tr. Thackeray, Loeb ed.
[3] Op. cit., pp. 106 f.

passage introducing the *Jewish Antiquities*, in which "hesitation and delay" were experienced by Josephus in the execution of so large a literary enterprise; moreover, the exact point is identified at which the delay took place, namely at the end of *Ant.* XIV. Thus, in effect, Thackeray maintains that the "assistants" started work at the beginning of *Ant.* XV, and at the end of *Ant.* XIV there was a break in the narrative. He mentions, incidentally, another reason to support the hypothesis of the use of "assistants", because especially in *Ant.* XVIII and XIX the sources were Latin documents: Josephus' "proficiency in Latin was even slighter"[1] (than his proficiency in Greek), so that an assistant was necessary.

The conclusion is correct, granting the validity of the premises, but it is here that further consideration is necessary. First, then, we must consider the "break" at the end of *Ant.* XIV, when interest is supposed to have flagged, and the beginning of *Ant.* XV, when the tale was taken up again. Secondly, we must consider the detailed grounds for positing the Sophoclean and Thucydidean assistants respectively.

1. THE END OF "ANT." XIV AND THE BEGINNING OF "ANT." XV

Book XIV opens with a short introduction, explaining that Josephus planned to narrate in that book the events following on the death of Queen Alexandra, and stating that his main purpose was "not to omit anything whether through ignorance or fault of memory" because truth was of primary importance in a historian's narrative.[2] The book ends with the capture of Jerusalem by Herod the Great and Sossius, and the execution of Antigonus, the last Hasmonean ruler. That there is a break in the narrative at the end of this book cannot be denied, for it is a turning point in the affairs of Herod, after which he gave attention to the consolidation of his gains and the strengthening of his position in Jerusalem. But it is a natural

---

[1] Op. cit., p. 109.   [2] Cf. also *B.J.* I. 16; *Ant.* I. 4.

break in the continuity of the narrative, which opens again at the beginning of *Ant.* XV and describes the next eighteen years up to the finishing of the Temple by Herod. With further evidence from the narrative itself, it seems somewhat arbitrary to identify the point at which "hesitation and delay" occurred with the end of *Ant.* XIV, and to conclude that Josephus then resorted to the expedient of employing assistants in the manner suggested by Thackeray.

The break may have been due to change of sources. If this is so, a stronger case could possibly be made out for hesitation and delay at that point. But what is the evidence? In *Ant.* XI and XII, the underlying sources are the Greek Esdras A,[1] Nehemiah,[2] Esther,[3] an account of Alexander the Great,[4] the so-called Letter of Aristeas,[5] and 1 Maccabees. [6] A big break comes when these Greek sources are no longer of use in Josephus' narrative, but from *Ant.* XIII. 212, Josephus' own *Jewish War* is used as a source, temporarily. When he reached *Ant.* XV, the History of Nicolaus of Damascus was available as a source.

There is ample direct evidence of this, for specific reference is made to this writer, who could be expected to write in favourable terms of his patron. To take two examples, the 123rd and 124th books of his History are mentioned,[7] and also a speech by Nicolaus in defence of the Jews.[8]

But in *Ant.* XV, where Nicolaus of Damascus is clearly used, it is not such a big break as might at first be imagined. For, from *Ant.* XIII. 212 onwards, as just mentioned, Josephus' own work is used also as a source, and it is clear that he too used Nicolaus in that work, so that Nicolaus is a source common to both the *Jewish War* and the *Antiquities*. It is therefore a matter of the extent to which Nicolaus was used as a source, and how far he was used directly in the *Antiquities*,

---

[1] *Ant.* XI. 1–c. 156.
[2] *Ant.* XI. 159–c. 180.
[3] *Ant.* XI. 186–c. 296.
[4] Cf. esp. *Ant.* XI. 313–47.
[5] *Ant.* XII. 11–118.
[6] *Ant.* XII. 240–XIII. 212.
[7] *Ant.* XIII. 127.
[8] *Ant.* XVI. 31–57.

or indirectly through the *Jewish War*. That he was used much more extensively in *Ant*. XV is clear.

Another subsidiary source used for *Ant*. XIII–XV is Strabo. Reference is made to his work three times in *Ant*. XIII,[1] four times in *Ant*. XIV,[2] and once in *Ant*. XV.[3] There is thus a considerable amount of continuity, rather than a break, which can be detected. Moreover, if the Sophoclean assistant was active to any great extent in *Ant*. XV, these references to Strabo indicate that when he took over from Josephus himself, he himself followed his methods very closely. Such a striking similarity in method might appear to indicate Josephus as sole author rather than support the hypothesis of an assistant, unless there is further very convincing evidence.

2. THE CASE FOR THE "SOPHOCLEAN" ASSISTANT ("ANT." XV–XVI)

Thackeray based his case upon "certain distinctive characteristics of style, and an affinity to a particular class of literature".[4] This Sophoclean assistant had a "love of Greek poetry, Sophocles in particular",[5] and drew on the *Ajax* and the *Electra* for words, phrases and reminiscences, e.g. the phrase ἀπὸ τοῦ στέγους διοπτεύειν in *Ant*. XV. 421;[6] κατὰ δ' ἡλιόυ βολάς;[7] ἐνώμοτος;[8] and ποῖ ποτ' οἴχονται σου αἱ φρένες;[9] and μῖσος ἐντετηκέναι.[10] This list was elaborated in *A Lexicon to Josephus*.[11] It must be candidly admitted that these words and phrases are most striking, and that some explanation must be found to account for them. Is it insufficient to say that Josephus himself may have been struck by these phrases? For it is clear that he studied Greek literature, which would include Sophocles, and not improbable that he himself introduced some Sophoclean phrases. Again, if a theory of a Sophoclean

---

[1] 286, 319, 347 (coupled with Nicolaus).
[2] 35, 68 (coupled with Nicolaus), 111, 138.　　　　[3] 9.
[4] Op. cit., p. 115.　　　　　　　[5] P. 116.
[6] Cf. Soph. *Aj*. 307.　　　　　[7] *Ant*. XV. 418, cf. *Aj*. 877.
[8] Ibid. 368, cf. *Aj*. 113.　　　[9] *Ant*.. XVI. 380, cf. *El*. 390.
[10] *Ant*. XVI. 33, cf. *El*. 1311.　　　[11] Part I, Intro., p. viii; Paris 1930.

assistant is based on the appearance of a special phrase like μῖσος ἐντετηκέναι, what is to be said when that very phrase occurs also in Dionysius of Halicarnassus?[1] One such case is not conclusive one way or another, but it weakens the case for the Sophoclean assistant still further.

The fact is that the Greek prose of the first century A.D., written and spoken, was much more of a combination of classical and poetical words and phrases; this is a characteristic, especially, of the Greek of the New Testament, but is by no means confined to it. It needs to be remembered that the works of Josephus were written within the same period as the New Testament writings. The case, therefore, for the Sophoclean assistant in *Ant.* XV–XVI is not made out sufficiently, especially when we bear in mind the *a priori* grounds against it.

Thackeray also cited examples from the *Jewish War* in support of his hypothesis. Here it is difficult to follow the logic of the argument, for if some words and phrases in *Ant.* XV–XVI are taken to support the theory of a Sophoclean assistant, similar words and phrases occurring elsewhere should result in the same inference. But, apparently, the same inference in this respect is not drawn, for while the theory seems to be that the Sophoclean assistant was responsible for *Ant.* XV–XVI, it is not held that he was responsible in the same way for parts, at least, of the *Jewish War*. There is therefore a distinction in the method of assistance in the *Jewish War* and the *Antiquities*. But on what grounds? In the absence of some positive supporting evidence on this point, the only possible course, logically, is to admit that the exact position is not clear, and that, in fact, we do not know it. Among the examples cited by Thackeray from the *Jewish War* are θράσος ὁπλίζειν,[2] ἀφειδεῖν ψυχῆς,[3] οὐδὲν ὑγιὲς φρονεῖν,[4] θάρσος προξενεῖν,[5] and ζῇ καὶ τέθηλε.[6] These words and phrases are admittedly striking, but, as has been suggested above, they are inconclusive in the Greek of this period. Moreover, such striking words

---

[1] *Ant. Rom.* VI. 93.   [2] *B.J.* III. 153.   [3] *B.J.* III. 212.
[4] *B.J.* V. 326; *Ant.* IX. 118.   [5] *B.J.* V. 66.   [6] *B.J.* VII. 348.

and phrases occur elsewhere in Josephus' works, e.g. *Ant.*
XIX. 145 πενθιμώτατα, but it points to the nature of first-
century Greek and Josephus' style, rather than to the work of
an assistant.

What conclusion is to be drawn from the occurrence of the
first person singular [1] on several occasions in *Ant.* XV and XVI?
If a Sophoclean assistant wrote these books, such references
have a special significance. In *Ant.* XVI. 174 παρεθέμην means
"I (Josephus) . . .",[2] and he writes as a Jew, as the passage
implies. Sometimes the *pluralis dignitatis* is used,[3] and it is
clearly such, as appears in *Ant.* XVI. 187 where a reference
follows to the royal Hasmonean house from which Josephus
claimed descent. The internal evidence provided by such
references is strong against the use of an assistant, at least in
those particular passages.

On the whole, therefore, after consideration of the evidence
adduced by Thackeray in favour of his hypothesis, the
arguments do not appear very strong. Internal evidence and
other considerations mentioned above weigh heavily against
his theory.

3. THE "THUCYDIDEAN" ASSISTANT IN "ANT." XVII–XIX

We have already stated the grounds on which Thackeray
based his theory of the Thucydidean assistant, who, he alleged,
took over from the Sophoclean assistant, and was responsible
for *Ant.* XVII–XIX: in the last book of the *Antiquities,* Josephus
himself took up the narrative again to add the final chapters.

What do we know of Josephus' proficiency in the Greek
language? This question is in a general way relevant to
this whole matter, for Thackeray's theory assumes a lack of
fluency which made composition difficult, so that Josephus
tired, for a time, of writing his *Antiquities.*

It is clear that Josephus had assistance with the *Jewish
War.*[4] This work was written at first in Aramaic, and later

---

[1] *Ant.* XVI. 174, 178, 404.   [2] The whole passage, 174–8, likewise.
[3] E.g. *Ant.* XVI. 187, 404.   [4] Cf. supra. *Contra Ap.* I. 50.

translated into Greek. But the precise manner in which Josephus used these assistants is not stated. It would seem improbable that *they* did the actual work of translation, for that would imply that they knew Aramaic as well as Greek: it is much more probably a matter of ascertaining, as far as possible, the facts about Josephus' progress in learning the Greek language.

The first occasion on which he needed Greek was during his first visit to Rome,[1] and even then he had with him a Jewish actor named Alityrus, who may have sometimes been his interpreter. Later, he was with the Romans as an interpreter at the siege of Jerusalem.[2] We may conclude therefore that at that time Josephus was not ignorant of Greek, but the spoken Greek with which he made himself understood is to be distinguished from literary composition. The *Jewish War* is, moreover, written in a polished style, for which, at that time, Josephus himself could not have been entirely responsible.

But when we turn to the *Antiquities*, an interval of about twenty years had elapsed, during which Josephus lived in Rome, and applied himself to the study of Greek literature.[3] He was not therefore labouring under the same difficulties, in about A.D. 90, with regard to the writing of Greek, as he admittedly was immediately after A.D. 70, so that his need of assistants had diminished, if not disappeared entirely, by the time he wrote the *Antiquities*. The case for the Thucydidean assistant is therefore weakened.

If, because of weariness and lack of fluency in the Greek language Josephus used assistants in the *Antiquities*, why did he not use them in the writing of the *Contra Apionem*? Even on Thackeray's admission, he did not avail himself of them for that work, written very soon after the *Antiquities*.

Where Josephus used assistants he says so, and from these general considerations it seems more reasonable to hold the view that the work of the assistants was a special characteristic

---

[1] In A.D. 64: *Life* 13–16.   [2] Captured A.D. 70.
[3] *Ant.* XX. 263. see also Note A, appended to this chapter.

of the *Jewish War*, though difficult to identify except for Josephus' own statement, and the fact that he admitted their
assistance in the *Jewish War*, thereby distinguishing it from
his subsequent works.

The ultimate test, however, is the style of *Ant.* XVII–XIX.
If it can be shown that in this respect these books are entirely
dissimilar to the others, the theory of an assistant responsible
for them finds support, in spite of general considerations to
the contrary; but if there are indications that the style of
these books is consistent with that of Josephus elsewhere, the
theory of an assistant becomes insupportable, and general
considerations lend their weight against it. In this examination
of the style of *Ant.* XVII–XIX, therefore, its characteristics
will be considered in some detail, and compared and contrasted
with the rest of the work, with special reference to *Ant.* XX
and the *Life*, which are agreed to be the products of Josephus'
own pen: next, an explanation will be offered which seems to
be most consistent with all the facts.

4. THE CHARACTERISTICS OF THE STYLE OF "ANT." XVII–XIX

(*a*) Direct reminiscences of the style of Thucydides are to
be found, as Thackeray pointed out.[1] Examples, some of
which he quotes, are οἱ ἀρετῆς τι μεταποιούμενοι (Thuc. II.
51. 5) found in *Ant.* XVIII. 20, 278, with variations in XVII.
153 (ὀριγνᾶσθαι) and XVII. 149, 181 (προσποίησις): δοξῇ
μᾶλλον ἀμαθεῖ ἢ προνοίᾳ ἀσφαλεῖ in XVII. 156, an echo of τὸ
δὲ πλέον βουλήσει κρίνοντες ἀσαφεῖ ἢ προνοίᾳ ἀσφαλεῖ (Thuc. IV.
108. 4). So too βοῇ καὶ διακελευσμῷ χρώμενοι in XVII. 216
may have been inspired by προθυμίᾳ τε πάσῃ χρώμενοι καὶ
παρακελευσμῷ (Thuc. IV. 11. 3). ἐπεκλάσθη τε τῇ διανοίᾳ
Ant. XVII. 74[2] is reminiscent of ἐπικλασθεῖεν τῇ γνώμῃ
(Thuc. III. 59. 1 and 67. 2). Similarly τοῦ μανιώδους in XVII.
215 echoes καὶ τοῦ Κλέωνος καίπερ μανιώδης οὖσα ἡ ὑπόσχεσις

---

[1] Op. cit., pp. 111 f.   [2] Cf. *Ant.* XVIII. 275.

ἀπέβη (Thuc. IV. 39. 3); the only other important reference to this word is in Euripides.[1]

(b) A form of meiosis found in Thuc. I. 138. 3, οὐκ ἀπήλλακτο, occurs fourteen times in these books; synonymous phrases based on the same model, e.g. οὐκ ἀποτετραμμένος, occur nine times. In the short passage XVII. 32–39 no less than five instances of οὐκ ἀπηλλαγμένος (ἀποτετραμμένος) occur. This characteristic is most striking.

(c) It would appear from Niese's edition that the Thucydidean σσ instead of the later Attic ττ was used, since the manuscripts preserve σσ in these books more frequently than elsewhere. The edition of Naber, however, shows a distinct preference for ττ in almost every case, without expressing reasons or stating the authority. There are ten cases where Naber retains the σσ form; Niese, on the other hand, has σσ in almost every case, with twenty-three exceptions where he retains the Attic ττ. In some cases it is clear that the manuscripts show no unanimity in the matter, e.g. κρειττόνων (Ant. XIX. 211, Niese), where κρεισσόνων is also found.[2]

(d) Thucydides used τό with the neuter singular of the present participle as an abstract noun, instead of the more usual τό with the infinitive, e.g. ἐν τῷ μὴ μελετῶντι (Thuc. I. 142. 8); τὸ μὲν δεδιός (I. 36. 1); μετὰ τοῦ δρωμένου (V. 102. 1); τοῦ ὑπαπιέναι πλέον ἢ τοῦ μένοντος (V. 9. 6), which is a combination of the two. The usage is also found in Sophocles,[3] and may be compared with the use of τό and the neuter of an adjective, e.g. τὸ δὲ ἀστάθμητον τοῦ μέλλοντος (Thuc. IV. 62. 4). In Ant. XVII–XIX this Thucydidean characteristic is copied in over sixty cases. The original construction, as found in Thucydides, is found in at least twenty-eight cases. There are, moreover, extensions of the Thucydidean construction, so that the neuter singular of the *future* or *aorist* participles is used with τό, and the genitive is added between the article and the participle as an indication of the agent, e.g. τὸ τῶν

---

[1] *Bacch.* 299. [2] MWExc (Niese, *ad. loc.*).
[3] *Ph.* 674, *Tr.* 196.

ἀδελφῶν μὴ ἐπικοινωνῆσον (*Ant.* XVII. 1); τὸ τοῦ Ἀγρίππα προβουλεῦσαν (XVIII. 148); τὸ μὴ μέτρῳ τῶν δωρεῶν προϊέμενον (XVIII. 145). The examples of the extensions of the original Thucydidean construction are in fact approximately as numerous as the examples of the original.

(*e*) Special words and phrases occur which can be paralleled with Thucydides, e.g. κουφίζω (Thuc. II. 44; VI. 34) is also to be found, with its compounds and derivative noun six times in these books; προκόπτω in the sense of "advance", "progress", occurs seven times in *Ant.* XVIII, also in Thuc. IV. 60; VII. 56: μεταπέμπω "send for" occurs six times in these books; Thucydides seems to use the active and middle voices indiscriminately;[1] the middle voice also occurs in *Ant.* XVIII. 237; forms of μεθίστημι are found nine times in the absolute sense of removal or death.[2] None of these words or special usages can be decisively attributed to Thucydides alone, so that their occurrence in Josephus cannot be taken to indicate dependence on him: κουφίζω, for example, is found in Thucydides, Sophocles, Euripides, and Plutarch. Similarly, the long periphrastic phrase οὐδὲν (μηδὲν) εἰς ἀναβολάς, ἀλλ' ἐκ τοῦ ὀξέος is found in full five times in these books. There may be an echo of εὐθὺς καὶ μὴ ἐς ἀναβολάς (Thuc. VII. 15), but the addition in Josephus of ἐκ τοῦ ὀξέος is of importance. Sometimes Josephus divides the phrase: οὐδὲν εἰς ἀναβολάς (three times), and ἐκ τοῦ ὀξέος (twelve times).

The following general characteristics may be distinguished and appended to the more particular items mentioned above:

(*f*) The use of the perfect or pluperfect tenses where an aorist may have been expected according to strict grammar and idiom; there are over fifteen cases in each of these books.

(*g*) Cases of participles not adequately connected and subordinated are frequent, and in two examples there is an unexpected tense: αἰσθόμενος . . . νομίζων (*Ant.* XVIII. 99); ταραχθεὶς . . . ὑπολαμβάνων (XVIII. 105).

(*h*) Participles sometimes occur, especially in genitive

---

[1] L. & S., v.s. μεταπέμπω.   [2] Cf. Eur. *Fr.* 558.

absolute clauses *after* the main verb, giving an impression of anti-climax, or at least an after-thought, e.g. . . . . πολλῶν διατριβόντων (XVII. 155).

(*i*) Connecting particles are sometimes entirely lacking, sometimes inadequate (e.g. τε or οὖν alone), sometimes put late in the sentence. The last two expedients can be paralleled in both Thucydides and Dionysius of Halicarnassus.

(*j*) ἐπί with an abstract noun is found about seventy times in three books alone: it is used to express purpose. In other expressions, too, abstract nouns are found which in classical Greek would have been expressed by more concrete constructions.

(*k*) The pleonastic use of the pluperfect tense with ἄν in the apodosis of a past conditional sentence with implication is found six times in these books. Strictly an aorist tense with ἄν would be expected in such cases.

5. A COMPARISON OF THE STYLE OF "ANT." XVII–XIX WITH THE REST OF THE WORK; WITH SPECIAL REFERENCE TO "ANT." XX AND "LIFE"

(*a*) Thucydidean words and echoes are noticeable in *Ant.* XVII–XIX; they are not so noticeable elsewhere in the work.

(*b*) The particular form of meiosis mentioned above does not occur to any extent in *Ant.* XX or *Life*, so that we cannot detect a parallel to the extreme case of *Ant.* XVII. 32–39, where no less than five instances are to be found. Such a special phenomenon needs a special explanation.

(*c*) Naber's edition has ττ in every case in *Ant.* XX and *Life*, except for γλῶσσαν in XX. 90, but Niese prefers the σσ form. The situation is therefore identical with *Ant.* XVII–XIX. If the theory of Thackeray is valid, and the form ττ adopted, it is to be inferred that a characteristic of the Thucydidean assistant is shared by Josephus himself in *Ant.* XX and the *Life*. A "slavish imitator" of Thucydides in *Ant.* XVII–XIX would have been expected to use the thoroughly Thucydidean ξ for σ, e.g. ξύν for σύν, and ἐς for εἰς.

6—S.I.J.

(d) Similarly, the use of τό and the neuter of the adjective or the present participle is not confined to *Ant.* XVII–XIX, e.g. τὸ τοῦ βασιλέως φιλοκάλον (XII. 59); τὸ λυποῦν . . . τὸ ὠφελῆσον (XIII. 151); πρὸς τὸ δοκοῦν (XIII. 295); τῷ μηδ' ἐκείνων φεισαμένῳ (XVI. 404). It would seem therefore that the same author was responsible for all of these phrases. There is, however, a complex extension of this usage which is noteworthy, namely, ὑπὲρ τοῦ ὑμετέρου μὴ ἀπολουμένου τοσούτων ὄντων (XVIII. 280). This unique phrase, apart from anything else, is surely one of the most awkward in any Greek author.

(e) With regard to the special words and phrases, μεθίστημι (and derivatives) is found also in *Life* 423, τῆς ἐκ τοῦ βίου μεταστάσεως, and provides further evidence of a link between *Ant.* XVII–XIX and the last part of this work.

(f) Each of the general characteristics mentioned previously in (b)–(i) is to be found in *Ant.* XVII–XIX, *Ant.* XX, and the *Life*, e.g. pleonastic use of the pluperfect with ἄν, *Ant.* XVII. 184, 275; XVIII. 181; XIX. 15, 262, 263; XX. 182; *Life* 96, 262, 343. The danger of agreeing with a theory such as that of the Thucydidean assistant is that the significance of such general characteristics may be minimized, and the presence of unusual characteristics magnified.

To summarize this investigation so far, it may be said that Thackeray's theory does not explain enough, and in effect ignores the characteristics common to *Ant.* XVII–XIX and the rest of the work, especially *Ant.* XX and the *Life*. But it has been admitted that some most unusual phrases and words occur for which a special explanation should be forthcoming. An attempt to provide such an explanation will follow a short reference to the style of Thucydides, which has of necessity been frequently mentioned, without any detailed examination.

"Thucydides was the natural standard of historical style."[1] Josephus certainly studied him.[2] There may therefore be

---

[1] Thackeray, op. cit., p. 110.   [2] Cf. *Ant.* XX. 263.

traces of Thucydides in any Greek historian, so that the need for a theory of an assistant is less necessary. Dionysius of Halicarnassus also studied Thucydides, and wrote an extant work on his style; he is one of the sources used by Josephus.

But what exactly characterizes the style of Thucydides? This question is complex, and does not admit of an easy answer, especially as large issues, such as the authenticity of the Periclean speeches, are bound up with it. Professor Finley's work, *Thucydides*,[1] only contains an attempted answer towards it: it is, he says,[2] "a style which, unlike that of Hecataeus, possesses the strongest possible means of emphasis and contrast within any given sentence, but which, unlike the periodic style, is normally somewhat rigid, because it tends to juxtapose rather than to subordinate". Clarity and elaboration are stated to be the marks of his "formal" style, in the speeches and descriptive passages. His diction was "by later standards both archaic and poetic".[3] His style is only to be understood "in the setting of the period".[4] Mr Lamb's work [5] investigated the matter more thoroughly, and at the end the author attempted a conclusion about his style.[6] His view is that "style, indeed, is like chaff blown about by the wind, if it be severed, either actually or in critical treatment, from the thought which has grown with it and within it to maturity".[7] Professor Gilbert Murray's opinion is quoted:[8] "Thucydides' style as it stands in our texts is an extraordinary phenomenon. Undeniably a great style, terse, restrained, vivid. . . . Undeniably also an artificial style, obscure amid its vividness, archaistic and poetic in vocabulary, and apt to run into verbal flourishes which seem to have little thought behind them." It is generally agreed that there are, as it were, two styles in Thucydides, that of the speeches, and that of the narrative.

[1] Oxford University Press, 1947.   [2] Pp. 254–5.
[3] Ibid. p. 266.   [4] P. 272.
[5] *Clio Enthroned: a study of prose-form in Thucydides.* Cambridge University Press, 1914.
[6] Chap. 10, Conclusion: section 3, pp. 312–14.
[7] P. 314.   [8] Pp. 4–5.

The connection between them constitutes one of the great problems in Thucydides; and the whole matter is complicated by the character of the historian himself, the style of his day, and his circumstances as a writer.

The temptation therefore is to be resisted to speak too glibly about the style of Thucydides, as though it were a simple and self-evident phenomenon. And if the theory of a Thucydidean assistant in *Ant.* XVII–XIX is accepted, then further details may well be required as to the method of this assistant's imitation of Thucydides' style, whether it is confined to the style of the Thucydidean speeches, or descriptive passages or narrative, or all of these, or some. This information is not forthcoming in the exposition of Thackeray's theory: it is a crucial omission, which while not invalidating the theory altogether, discredits it to the extent of rendering it much less plausible and cogent.

Having rejected this theory, however, we are left with the task of explaining the presence of some most unusual words and phrases in *Ant.* XVII–XIX. It is insufficient to say that *Ant.* XVII–XIX are the work of Josephus: such an explanation errs towards the opposite extreme of not explaining enough.

These peculiarities seem on the whole to become less striking after reaching their peak approximately half-way through *Ant.* XVIII, e.g. τῆς ψυχῆς τὸ θέλον (XVIII. 144); τὸ μὴ μέτρῳ τῶν δωρεῶν προϊέμενον (147); τό τ'ἐπὶ τοιούτοις τοῦ 'Αγρίππα προβουλεῦσαν (148). After that, although the most bizarre phrase ὑπὲρ τοῦ ὑμετέρου μὴ ἀπολουμένου τοσούτων ὄντων occurs in XVIII. 280, the peculiarities become less frequent, and by the time we reach *Ant.* XIX, the style is very much that of *Ant.* XX and the *Life*.

The explanation may be that Josephus took a phrase, worked upon it, and extended it, in a comparatively short space, and then discarded it. For example, προύκοπτε occurs seven times in *Ant.* XVIII, but not in XVII or XIX: ἐν (or ἐπ') ἀπογνώσει τινος is found three times [1] between the middle of *Ant.* XVIII and XIX. Josephus seems to have a word or phrase uppermost in his mind for a while, then it gives way to another with which he happens to be familiar, or which for the moment appeals to him. Such a phenomenon is not rare: Livy is prone to use an awkward expression several times within the course of a few pages, and then drop it. When Josephus had worked one word or phrase enough, another took its place: when the use of the violent extension of the Thucydidean τό with the neuter singular of the present participle becomes less frequent, the use of προύκοπτε emerges; when this begins to wane, ἐν (or ἐπ') ἀπογνώσει begins to appear.

Whether the process was conscious or unconscious is irrelevant to the explanation of the phenomenon as such. It is indeed possible that the process took place in the course of the revision of his work for a second edition.[2] Whatever be the facts of that particular case, where conjecture is alone, at present, permissible, they do not affect this suggested explanation of the peculiarities of *Ant.* XVII–XIX.

Thackeray's theory of the Thucydidean assistant is superficially attractive, but basically unsound; fuller consideration renders it improbable and unnecessary.

NOTE A

JOSEPHUS AND GREEK LITERATURE: "ANT." XX. 258 ff.

This is an illuminating passage which serves as a conclusion to the *Antiquities*. After making a claim to accuracy in his narrative, (262) Josephus proceeds to produce reasons in support of that claim:

(*a*) his fellow-Jews admitted his expert and indeed superior knowledge of his native literature,

[1] XVIII. 285; XIX. 99; XIX. 248.
[2] See note B appended to this chapter.

and moreover

> (b) "with much diligence he took pains to become conver-
> sant in (lit. share) Greek prose and poetry, having
> memorized grammatical experience" (Ant. XX. 263).

Such is the literal translation of the participial clause τὴν
γραμματικὴν ἐμπειρίαν ἀναλαβών, which is crucial to Josephus'
statement, but difficult to translate accurately. Indeed, it
seems to be slurred over in some translations. ἀναλαβών can
hardly mean anything else except "having memorized" (see
Liddell and Scott, new edition). The participle is used to
describe an action subsequent to that of the main verb
ἐσπούδασα ("I took pains"): such a usage is not unheard of
in earlier Greek and is found elsewhere in Josephus (Ant. XX.
204, διαφθείρας). So ἀναλαβών is to be translated "and thus
(later) I memorized . . .". What Josephus intended to convey
is that he studied Greek literature, prose and poetry, and by
that means mastered and committed to memory the rules of
grammar and syntax which he there found illustrated. This
is precisely what would be necessary for anyone proceeding to
the written composition of a language hitherto only used in
conversation, for in conversation inadequate grammar and
syntax may pass muster, but not in composition.

He then proceeded to mention the matter of pronunciation,
which did not, of course, affect adversely his written style,
while causing some difficulty, alleging that accuracy with
regard to pronunciation was prevented by the Jewish national
habit of valuing more highly than the mere ability to speak
languages, the ability to know and interpret the Jewish
scriptures. The reason alleged, incidentally, does not sound
very convincing.

Taking all these statements together, and noting also
Josephus' own statement elsewhere (Life 9) that he was a man
of talents and education, we have sufficient material for a
picture of his progress in learning the Greek language.

It is also worthy of note that this very revealing passage

was probably added to the end of the *Antiquities* for its second edition, when the *Life* was added, attacking and refuting Justus of Tiberias. Justus himself claimed to be conversant in Greek literature (*Life* 40) and diligent (φιλόπονος, *Life* 338); in this passage Josephus showed his own familiarity with Greek literature and, incidentally, said that he himself took much pains over its study.

Note B

On the second edition of the "Jewish Antiquities"

The *Jewish Antiquities* and the *Life* were meant to form an integral whole: the latter was written after A.D. 100, because in *Life* 359 the death of Agrippa II is assumed, which occurred, according to Photius, in A.D. 100. The *Jewish Antiquities* contains two separate endings, at XX. 259 and XX. 267, the latter giving the date A.D. 94, i.e. the thirteenth year of Domitian. What is the explanation?

It is quite possible that there was a second edition published, together with the *Life*, after A.D. 100. The presence of the two endings is due, not so much to carelessness on the part of Josephus, as to the impossibility of making the necessary alterations in all the copies of the first edition; so the work came to be circulated with the additions of the second edition, but without the deletions intended for the second edition.

So much it seems reasonable to infer, but it may also be *conjectured* that some of the peculiarities of *Ant.* XVII–XIX were inserted in a second edition of the work: one phrase was used frequently for a time, only to give way to another. The most difficult question in connection with this is—why did Josephus choose those particular books for revision, in preference to others? A hint may be found in the subject matter of these books. In *Ant.* XVII, the death of Herod is reached (XVII. 191) so that a change of source would be necessary. Josephus may have felt, when the time came for a second edition, that the narrative following on the death of Herod may have needed revision; hence the rather clumsy attempts at the revision of the style, which, from one point of view, he would have been well advised not to have attempted. But perhaps even so we can see the justification for it from Josephus' point of view, without agreeing with it: Justus was an expert on style, and the *Life* was a refutation of Justus' attack on Josephus. The *Life* refutes Justus' claims to accuracy, and was added to the *Jewish Antiquities*, second edition. To refute any accusation of Justus on the score of style, Josephus may have polished the style of *Ant.* XVII–XIX for the second edition, with unfortunate results.

CHAPTER 5

THE "JEWISH ANTIQUITIES"
with special reference to Josephus' style

A. JOSEPHUS AND NICOLAUS OF DAMASCUS

APART from passing references to other authors, which of themselves would suffice for a broad outline, we possess in addition considerable portions of Nicolaus' *Autobiography*:[1] there is missing a short portion (p. 418) near the beginning, and towards the end (p. 422) there are two pages not now extant. According to Nicolaus, his father Antipater and his mother Stratonice were highly esteemed wealthy citizens of Damascus, with two sons, Ptolemaeus and Nicolaus. Antipater gave his promising son Nicolaus a very complete education:[2] before he arrived at manhood, he was far ahead of his school-fellows, showing a particular bent for "grammar and poetry". He even composed tragedies and comedies, besides applying himself to "rhetoric, music, mathematics, and all philosophy". He was an Aristotelean, but did not use his philosophical learning to gain money. At this point comes the first gap in the *Life*, and the narrative is resumed with an account of his successful pleading on behalf of Ilium, the inhabitants of which had been heavily fined by M. Agrippa for not assisting his wife Julia, who was almost drowned attempting to cross the swollen waters of the Scamander. Nicolaus was evidently there with Herod, who was at that time studying philosophy with him. Later Herod took up rhetoric for a time, until his whim changed to the

---

[1] Nic. Dam. *Hist. Graec. Frag.*, ed. Orelli. Leipzig 1804, containing an essay by M. Sevin, "*Recherches sur Nicolas de Damas*".

[2] ἐν τῇ ὅλῃ παιδείᾳ τετραμμένος, p. 414.

study of history. It was Herod, says Nicolaus, who begged
him to write history on such a scale that Hercules himself
would have failed, if Eurystheus had set it him. When Herod
visited Rome, Nicolaus accompanied him, and together they
studied philosophy.[1] Nor was the manner of life of this versatile teacher inconsistent with the doctrines he taught, in spite
of his converse with royalty; his tastes were frugal. The
narrative is here interrupted with a considerable lacuna, and
resumes with the objections brought against Nicolaus, firstly
that he had won undeserved glory from Herod, secondly that
he did not save large fortunes with which he was presented,
and that he conversed with his social inferiors. Both of these
charges Nicolaus vigorously rebuts philosophically, and ends
his *Life* with the statement that he educated his slaves and
treated them as friends and equals, much in the manner of
Horace.

Thus the autobiography of Nicolaus tells of his accomplishments, and the high position which he gained at the
court of Herod the Great, and even with Augustus. Constantinus Porphyrogenitus (A.D. 912–59), to whom we owe
directly the preservation of such works of Nicolaus as we
have, calls him Herod's "secretary", a general term meaning
confidant, courtier, teacher, and friend. This broad outline
is confirmed and expanded in some detail with references in
other authors. Sophronius (fl. 7th cent. A.D.) says that Nicolaus
was the tutor of the children of Antony and Cleopatra, and,
according to Strabo,[2] he saw the Indian ambassadors who
came to Antioch during Augustus' visit to Syria. Josephus
mentions his championing of the Jews,[3] although he himself
was not a Jew; the embassy on which he was sent by Herod
against Archelaus[4] of Cappadocia and his attempt to reconcile
Augustus and Herod[5] by attacking Syllaeus and the Arabians;
his part in the accusation of Antipater by Herod;[6] his speech

---

[1] καὶ κοινῇ ἐφιλοσόφουν, p. 421.   [2] XV. 1. 73.
[3] *Ant.* XVI. 29–58.   [4] *Ant.* XVI. 332 ff.
[5] *Ant.* XVI. 338.   [6] *Ant.* XVII. 99, 110–26.

for Archelaus before Augustus in the deliberations resulting in the establishment of tetrarchies after the death of Herod.[1]

Athenaeus [2] illustrates his close relationship with Augustus (ἑταίρου ὄντος αὐτῷ), mentioning that the Emperor honoured Nicolaus, who sent him choice dates from Syria, by calling them after him. Eustathius (fl. c. A.D. 1160) quotes the passage, and Plutarch mentions it,[3] incidentally, in explanation, describing Nicolaus as γλυκὺν ὄντα τῷ ἤθει, ῥαδινὸν δὲ τῷ μήκει τοῦ σώματος, διάπλεων δὲ τὸ πρόσωπον ἐπιφοινίσσοντος ἐρυθήματος. Suidas in his Lexicon, under Nicolaus, quotes the main points from the *Life*.

These notices, altogether, give a reasonably full account of Nicolaus' life, though we have no chronological system given. He was a contemporary of Herod the Great, and survived him, writing of the Emperor Augustus and living therefore up to A.D. 14 at least. If he was tutor to Cleopatra's children, he would probably have been born before 60 B.C., his death taking place before A.D. 20. We may also assume that he came into Herod's employ after Actium, i.e. about 30 B.C. Nicolaus himself mentions his detractors, suggesting thereby that even in his life-time his career did not please all, some evidently thinking him merely a flatterer and a time-server first of Cleopatra and Antony, then of Herod and Augustus. Such attacks would doubtless chiefly come from the opponents of Herod. The position which Nicolaus held at Herod's side would inevitably cause dissatisfaction by the very reason of its conspicuousness, and there are still similar charges levelled against him. Orelli[4] calls him "*adulatorum vilissimus et gratiae potentiorum studiosissimus auceps*", and compares him with Velleius Paterculus. Nicolaus would no doubt have preferred to be compared with his master Aristotle; but, admittedly, it was no mean accomplishment to have attained to such a position of trust, and dislike for Herod should not thereby

---

[1] *Ant.* XVIII. 219, 240–7.   [2] XIV. 652.
[3] *Symp. Probl.* 8. 4.   [4] Op. cit., Preface.

involve dislike for his friends. Nicolaus was a man of many
varied achievements: as rhetorician, "musician", philosopher,
poet, dramatist, statesman, politician, and historian, he
possessed a versatility of which he had some reason to be
proud. He is guilty at times of exaggeration (e.g. in describing
his history as too big a task for a labour of Hercules) but that
is rather due to rhetoric than intentional misrepresentation:
it is also in the *Life* that he mentions his frugality and care for
slaves. Nicolaus must have acquiesced in, if not agreed with,
the policies of Herod and Augustus, and, before that, though
perhaps in a less degree, of Cleopatra. These policies may have
been sometimes directly opposed to one another.

His works. Thanks to Porphyrogenitus we now possess some
portions of the works of Nicolaus. His *Autobiography* has been
mentioned above. He also wrote a large history. Athenaeus [1]
states that it was in 144 books, while Suidas [2] states "he
wrote a general history in 80 books". The fragments which
we now possess prove that Suidas is wrong, though only 80
books may have been known to Suidas himself. There is a
considerable portion of Book 1 surviving, also of 6 and 7.
Josephus mentions Book 4 (*Ant.* I. 159, VII. 101), as do
Stephanus Byzantius and Constantinus Porphyrogenitus:
Josephus also refers to Books 96 (*Ant.* I. 94), 123, and 124
(XII. 127). Reference to Books 5 and 9 is also found in
Stephanus, to Book 18 in Porphyrogenitus, and to Books
104, 107, 108, 110, 114, and 116 in Athenaeus. This evidence
is conclusive against Suidas. The work was a universal history
as the references show: the surviving portions of Book 1 deal
with the Kings of Assyria, the labours of Hercules, and the
mythical Kings of Lydia and Lycia. Periander of Corinth is
dealt with after the sixth book, and the Kings of Lydia,
Gyges, Alyattes, and Croesus; then come Cyrus and the
Persian Kings, leading up to the legends of early Rome, ending
the seventh book. There is a large element of myth recounted
in this early history, which is comparable with that which

---

[1] VI. p. 249.   [2] V.s. Νικόλαος.

was written by Livy and Dionysius of Halicarnassus in the
same age. The period, then, with which the *Universal History*
deals is from the earliest times to the establishment of the
tetrarchies by Augustus after the death of Herod in 4 B.C.
There is no actual evidence for this final statement; but since
books 123 and 124 deal with Nicolaus' petition before M.
Agrippa on behalf of the Jews in 14 B.C. (*Ant.* XII. 127),
there are still twenty books in which to bring the narrative
up to the tetrarchs. This is further supported by the abrupt
change in Josephus' narrative towards the end of *Ant.* XVII,
signifying a change in the source, which had been, on all
showing, Nicolaus' history. The *Life of Augustus* is preserved
almost in its entirety, containing fifteen chapters. It is much
in the nature of a court panegyric, but contains much of
value in spite of that. Suetonius is supposed to have used it as a
source for his *Life of Augustus*, according to one theory.
Photius [1] says Nicolaus compiled a παραδόξων ἔργων συναγωγή.
It is known to us only at second hand, through Stobaeus.
Eustathius mentions a tragedy, *Susanna*, which Nicolaus
published; beyond the name, however, we know nothing of it.
Stobaeus preserves about fifty lines from a comedy, describing
parasites.[2] The titles of some minor philosophical works remain, but no philosophical treatise survives which can with
certainty be attributed to Nicolaus. From these notices of
his works it may be inferred that Nicolaus was a man of parts,
a prolific and versatile writer who found opportunity for
composition in the midst of court life.

A parallel with Josephus at once springs to mind. Both left
their native cities, and both were historians; in fact, the
similarity of parts of the *Life* of both these authors, suggests
a priori interdependence; both, we hear, were youths "of

---

[1] *Biblioth. Cod.* 189.
[2] E.g.:

> τὸ τῶν παρασίτων ἐξεῦρε γένος
> Διὸς πεφυκώς, ὡς λέγουσι, Τάνταλος,
> οὐ δυνάμενος δὲ τῇ τύχῃ χρῆσθαι καλῶς,
> Ἀκόλαστον ἔσχε γλῶσσαν κτλ.

precocious talents", and good parentage; both, after a precarious start, became confidants of Emperors and client-Kings; both were attacked bitterly for it, and rebutted these charges in the *Autobiography* which each wrote.

There are, however, besides this general parallel, signs of direct use of Nicolaus' works by Josephus as a basis for his own. An author of a general history of the Jews from the Creation would, not without reason, go to the author of a universal history, who was intimately connected moreover with the King who changed the fortunes of Jerusalem so much. This Josephus did, as the numerous references to Nicolaus testify. Some have been given above. And to these may be added *Ant.* XIII. 250, 347; XIV. 68, 104; XVI. 183; *Contra Ap.* II. 84; *Ant.* I. 94, 107, 159; VII. 101. Thus there are references to him throughout the *Antiquities*, from which it may be inferred that Josephus had Nicolaus' history at hand, to supplement and confirm [1] his own statements and those found in his sources, that is, mainly the Hebrew Scriptures, for the early books. But at the point where Josephus approaches the rise of Herod to kingship, Nicolaus apparently becomes his main authority. The comparatively long space (three books, *Ant.* XV–XVII) which Josephus devotes to Herod is highly suggestive of this, besides the references themselves to Nicolaus. When Josephus ceased using 1 Maccabees as a source in *Ant.* XIII, his account becomes distinctly meagre and scanty in comparison until about the middle of *Ant.* XIV, and after the account of the arrangements after Herod's death (*Ant.* XVII), the change of source necessitated by the finishing of Nicolaus' history at this point causes a striking change in the narrative, which degenerates in *Ant.* XVIII into a disconnected patch-work.

[1] A favourite way of introducing a reference is μάρτυς δὲ τούτων ἡμῖν ἐστί (*Ant.* XIII. 250), or a similar form.

Josephus' use of Nicolaus, especially in Ant. *XV–XVII*
(reign of Herod: 37–4 *B.C.)*

It may be taken as certain that Josephus used Nicolaus in these books.[1] Taking the subsidiary sources first, we find that Josephus compiled his narrative with reference to Strabo's *Historical Work*, written before his extant *Geography*, and quoted in *Ant*. XIV. 68, 111, 119, 138; *Ant*. XV. 9 and 10. In *Ant*. XV. 174 there is a reference to the *Memoirs* of Herod. Schürer[2] believes that the acquaintance of Josephus with these "Commentaries or Memoirs" is at second hand, and cites the Imperfect Tense περιείχετο as evidence "that the work did not then lie before the writer". That such stress can be laid on the form of a word, on the assumption of exact use of tenses in Josephus, seems to be disproved by his careless uses of tenses in verbs and participles. In writing these *Memoirs*, Herod was following the example of Augustus; we may conjecture that it was at the suggestion of Nicolaus that he undertook it, and since Herod was, according to the *Life* of Nicolaus, interested in history, he probably welcomed the suggestion of his tutor to practise on a subject most congenial to himself. Doubtless, too, Nicolaus helped much in its compilation. Another source is posited sometimes,[3] namely a biography of Herod by "Ptolemy". Ammonius, *De Adfinium Vocabulorum Differentia*, quotes the first book of the Life of King Herod, under the heading of the difference between Idumean and Jew, stating that they are not the same. Evidently then the writer of this statement was not a partisan with a bias towards Herod, as Nicolaus was, according to Josephus.[4] This precludes the possibility either that the Ptolemaeus in question was Nicolaus' brother (cf. *Ant*. XVII. 225 φίλων . . . ʽΗρώδῃ τιμιώτατον), or that he was the

[1] Thackeray, *Josephus the Man and the Historian*, p. 66: "The main source is undoubtedly the History of Nicolas of Damascus."
[2] *The Jewish People in the time of Jesus Christ*, Div. I, vol. I, p. 56.
[3] E.g. in *Camb. Anc. Hist.*, vol. X, p. 886.
[4] *Ant*. XIV. 9.

Ptolemaeus "entrusted with Herod's seal" (*Ant.* XVII. 195). And so the work has been ascribed to Ptolemaeus of Ascalon, a grammarian. Schürer [1] points out that the dating of Ptolemaeus of Ascalon in Stephanus of Byzantium is about 210 B.C. He says he was Ἀρίσταρχος γνώριμος, i.e. Aristarchus the grammarian, but that this is generally discredited. It is tempting to conjecture that Josephus saw this work, particularly as the statement in *Ant.* XIV. 8, 9 agrees with that attributed to Ptolemaeus by Ammonius, but the confused chronology makes it difficult to speak convincingly of the conjecture. In any case, the rival claims of Idumean and Jew with regard to their original stock must have been known to Josephus apart from any specific authority.

From Nicolaus of Damascus himself, we may identify passages which could hardly come from anyone else. Since Cleopatra once employed Nicolaus as a tutor to her children, and later cast envious eyes upon Herod's kingdom, having dreams of the old Ptolemaic empire, we may take it that the accounts of these events [2] come from the man who had been with them both. It is doubtful whether all of this latter passage can be looked upon as history; such statements as those in *Ant.* XV. 97 may have a historical background, embellished with details from his own imagination and the gossip of the time. So great is the dependence of Josephus upon Nicolaus supposed to be, that it is even stated [3] that "much of his style here (*Ant.* XIV–XVII) probably reproduces that of Nicolaus". There are actual references to Nicolaus himself, which though not always agreeing with him, show, at least, that he was consulted.

Ant. XIV. 8 and 9: Josephus rebuts the statement of Nicolaus that Antipater was a Jew of noble birth (γένος ἐκ τῶν πρώτων Ἰουδαίων), saying that this was said to please (χαριζόμενος) Herod, Antipater's son.

---

[1] *The Jewish People in the time of Jesus Christ*, Div. I, vol. I, p. 57.
[2] E.g. *Ant.* XIV. 324; XV. 6 ff: *B.J.* I. 359 ff. *Ant.* XV. 88–110 (esp.).
[3] *Camb. Anc. Hist.*, vol. X. p. 870.

Ant. XVI. 183-6 (end): *À propos* of Herod's visit to the tomb of David, when in financial difficulties, Josephus mentions his propitiatory dedication, and says that Nicolaus mentions the dedication, but not the visit, implying intentional misleading of readers. Josephus also describes the account of the death of Mariamne and her sons in Nicolaus, justifying Herod, and explains both on the ground of his familiarity with Herod, and that he was writing an encomium on Herod, and "zealously defending his crimes", an offence only pardonable because the history of Nicolaus was ὑπουργίαν τῷ βασιλεῖ (186). Josephus then contrasts his own policy of putting truth before feelings, although he had great respect for many of Herod's descendants (187); but this passage may possibly have been written after A.D. 100, when Agrippa II was dead.

Ant. XV. 150 ff; XVI. 365-404. Both these passages contain a criticism of Herod; the first of Herod only, and the second of his sons Alexander and Aristobulus also, whom he executed.

It must be admitted that these passages either contain a direct criticism of Nicolaus, or have such an implication: although for example, Nicolaus is himself not mentioned by name in *Ant.* XVI. 395 ff, the passage, criticizing as it does Herod's family, must differ from the account which the history of Nicolaus, being favourable to Herod, would have given. Such passages, then, and indeed the whole account of Herod in *Ant.* XV–XVII, stand in direct contrast with that in *B.J.*[1] The two versions are by no means of equal length; that of *Ant.* XV–XVII being considerably longer, and, even of disproportionate length, considering the subject and nature of the work. It is also told chronologically, whereas the *B.J.* version makes a rough distinction between the public and private life of Herod, and the whole story is worked up almost like a tragedy.[2] As such then it is probably much more close

---

[1] *B.J.* I. 195-670, a sketch of his whole career.
[2] Cf. Thackeray, op. cit., p. 65.

to the original work of Nicolaus, who amongst his other
accomplishments wrote tragedies, and would be quick to
notice analogies for possible "tragic" subjects. There is not
in the *B.J.* account any such outspoken criticism of Herod,
as in the *Antiquities*.

There have been several attempts to explain the origin of
these divergent accounts. Hölscher [1] maintains that the main
source of Josephus in *Ant.* XV–XVII was not Nicolaus
himself, but a biased Jewish redactor, or a direct "falsifier"
of Nicolaus,[2] his views being anti-Herodian and violently
pro-Hasmonean. A somewhat similar view, though not so
far-reaching, is found in Schürer,[3] who says: "Josephus follows
Nicolaus as his chief authority, and besides him used only a
source that was unfavourable to Herod." In direct opposition
to this is the view of Laqueur,[4] that the career of Josephus
is one of "*Entwicklung*", especially in his point of view. He
compares *Ant.* XIV in detail with the *B.J.* account, and concludes that the *Antiquities* is correcting the *B.J.* version. By
about A.D. 90, he claims, Josephus had changed his opinion
of the Herods, taking now rather the nationalist Jewish
point of view, which opposed Rome and the Herods, and
approximated rather to the more orthodox view which Josephus a priest, a Pharisee, and a Hasmonean, would normally
be expected to take. But Laqueur goes on to state that Josephus at the same time made insertions into the *B.J.*, showing
his new policy, and that Josephus' source in *Ant.* XV ff has
"nothing to do either with his *B.J.* or with Nicolaus of
Damascus".

These then are the two views. Laqueur emphasizes an
important point in saying that the "evolution" of Josephus
has to be reckoned with. With a man like Josephus, who, to
judge from events in Galilee, was not of fixed and stable
principles, such changes later on in life would be not un-

---

[1] Pauly-Wissowa *Real-Enc.*, v.s. "Josephus".
[2] He calls him "*Nikolaosfälscher*".   [3] Op. cit., Div. I, vol. I. p. 56.
[4] *Der jüd. Hist. Fl. Jos.—passim.*

expected, especially if events had removed any obstacles which stood in the way. Such a theory too allows for the human element in the composition of history, which, even though it is sometimes to be deplored, cannot be ignored entirely. But Laqueur seems to go too far when he works out this theory with *Ant.* XIV and *B.J.*, proceeding to show signs of inter-connection, on a partial analogy with the "*Rechenschaftsbericht*" and the *Life*. His view, however, that the source of *Ant.* XV–XVII has nothing to do with the *B.J.*, or with Nicolaus, is unusual, and seems to disregard the important references to Nicolaus by name in these books.

While evolving his theory, Laqueur makes a quotation from Juster,[1] showing how common is the view that everything in Josephus comes straight from his sources without criticism: "Les Antiquités, dans la partie qui nous intéresse (i.e. the last books) valent en général ce que valent ses sources." This is, in effect, the view of Hölscher. Such a view assumes that Josephus had no critical powers, or did not use them, in writing his history, his general method being to give a paraphrase of the various sources he had before him. There is, however, considerable evidence that he not only possessed but used critical acumen: he points out where he disagrees with authors, and his reason for so doing (*Ant.* XIV. 138 ff); he quotes authors in support of his statements (XIII. 347; XIV. 68, Strabo, Nicolaus, and Livy); divergencies between authorities are stated and weighed (XIV. 119, Strabo and Crassus); the whole tenor of the *Life* is to maintain that Josephus sought after "truth" (cf. *Life* 336–67) especially, and employed all possible means for obtaining it. Josephus was not then an entirely uncritical historian, as some would have us believe, and it therefore seems improbable that in *Ant.* XV–XVII also the passages which disagree with Nicolaus should come not from Josephus, but from a "*Nikolaosfälscher*", as Hölscher suggests. The characteristically German study of "*Quellenkritik*" can be carried too far, if

---

[1] Jean Juster, *Les juifs dans l'Empire romain*, pp. 12 f.

there is a tendency to forget that the historian himself may well have made statements arising from personal convictions.

The more reasonable view then seems to be that Nicolaus was the main source for *Ant.* XV–XVII, with Strabo, the Commentaries of Herod, and, less probably, the Life of Herod by Ptolemaeus of Ascalon. It remains to be seen how the passages in criticism of Nicolaus came about. Josephus had been connected with Agrippa II at least from Jotapata to the fall of Jerusalem (A.D. 70), in somewhat the same way as Nicolaus was in close relationship with Herod the Great. It would be perhaps expected then that the *B.J.* and the *Ant.*, being based on Nicolaus, would not possess anything derogatory to Herod. But evidently the passages mentioned are exceptions: *Ant.* XIV. 9, for example, belongs to a time when Josephus did not believe that Herod was truly a Jew, and did not hold the highest opinion of him. Now the *Life* is known to have been written after A.D. 100, and there are two distinct endings in *Ant.* XX, so that at the same time as the *Life* a second edition of the *Antiquities* may well have been brought out. The date would then be after A.D. 100, when Agrippa was dead, and then Josephus could speak more freely the views to which he had perhaps changed in the last few years; what more probable then that these passages of criticism of Herod and Nicolaus may have been inserted in the second edition of the *Antiquities*, after the death of Agrippa II? The inconsistencies to which two different views expressed in the same book would give rise do not appear to have met with the consideration of Josephus, who, similarly, left two distinct endings to *Ant.* XX. The passages may well have been inserted in a second edition; their position is not such as to make this well-nigh impossible: e.g. the passage in *Ant.* XVI. 395–404 is at the end of the book and could easily have been added later. It is noticeable in this connection that none of the Latin manuscripts of Josephus possess this passage, a fact which may indicate subsequent addition.

If the foregoing explanation of the sources of *Ant.* XV-XVII is correct, Josephus used Nicolaus in the main, supplemented by other sources; but after A.D. 100 when Agrippa, one of his patrons, was dead, he inserted into a second edition of the *Antiquities* his own sincere personal views of Herod and Nicolaus. Perhaps, too, the composition of the *Contra Apionem*, in which Josephus championed Judaism against Hellenism, is indicative of this change of attitude on his part, which culminated later in the second edition of the *Antiquities*. Such an explanation involves us in the view that Josephus was guilty of "suppressing the truth" in A.D. 94, owing to the particular circumstances in which he was placed. In Josephus' favour it can be said that it must have been hard for him to do otherwise: a break with Agrippa, which a candid and sincere estimate of Herod's character would have caused, would doubtless have meant at Rome the loss of his pension and house. It would scarcely have endeared him entirely to the hearts of all Jews, who would be quick to remember Jotapata and Galilee. This must have been a dilemma for Josephus, and he chose the line of least resistance, ensuring his personal security by keeping in favour with Agrippa II at all costs. It is not to be inferred that Josephus never gave a hint of his personal feelings: *Ant.* XVII. 27, 28 (especially ἐξετρύχωσαν) imply a criticism. And this role of "suppressor of the truth" ill befitted Josephus, who was eager to know the truth himself and to write it. This gives additional point to the rather lengthy digressions on "truth" in *Ant.* XVI. 183–6 and *Life* 339 ff. If both of these passages were written after A.D. 100 (death of Agrippa)— and there is indisputable evidence for the last, and probability for the first—they are, as it were, a defence of the changes in his attitude. Josephus, who suppressed his true feelings originally, felt conscience-smitten about having done so. With the death of Agrippa and the antagonistic history of Justus as incentives, and feeling that Justus' attack was *partly* justified, he wrote "what had hitherto been suppressed" (*Life* 338),[1]

---

[1] τὰ μέχρι νῦν σεσιωπημένα.

and took care, in self-defence, to point out the reason for
his action, the absolute claims of truth upon a historian.

B. JOSEPHUS AND DIONYSIUS OF HALICARNASSUS

1a. *His life and writings*

The known details of the life of Dionysius of Halicarnassus
are meagre, and we have to rely mostly upon references in
his works. But, not being the sort of man to talk over-much of
himself, nor having a subject in which he himself played a
part, he makes few references to himself. The date of his birth
is usually given at about 60 B.C., when the Roman Republic
was in its death-throes. He was thus born at Halicarnassus
about four centuries after Herodotus, his fellow-townsman.
Nothing is known of his early life except that he became a
rhetorician. He went to live in Rome, "at the time when the
Civil War was brought to an end by Augustus Caesar"[1]—i.e.
about 30 B.C. The exact reason is not known, but it can be
assumed with probability that it was no political one: the
unique position which Rome was gaining as mistress of a wide
empire and the centre of the then known world is sufficient
to explain her attraction to Greeks, and more especially to
Greek rhetoricians. Later, if we can trust Juvenal, the city was
overcrowded with these "hungry Greeklings". We may
assume then that Dionysius had an academy in Rome, where
he taught rhetoric both in its original sense of the art of public
speaking, and its natural corollary, of the art of composing
speeches, that is, style. Several of his works on style have
come down: *On the Ancient Orators* is a series of six essays of
which we possess three, on Lysias, Isaeus, and Isocrates, and
essays on Demosthenes and Thucydides, all showing experience in literary criticism. He took care when he was in Rome,
he says,[2] to learn the Roman language, in addition to the
native Greek he spoke, and made himself "thoroughly acquainted with the national records". He lived then in Rome for

---

[1] Dion. Hal., *Ant. Rom.* I. 7.   [2] Ibid.

over twenty years,[1] working on material for the *Roman Antiquities*, a history of Rome in twenty books, from the earliest times down to 264 B.C.[2] The work was published about 8 B.C.[3] We possess the first ten books in full, most of the eleventh, and fragments only of the rest. His purpose in writing this history was to show his gratitude to the city of his adoption "for the education and other blessings which he received during his sojourn therein".[4] The date of his death is not known, but it was probably about ten years or so after the publication of this work.

1b. Dionysius as a man and as a writer

His purpose in writing the history, Dionysius says himself, was also "to reveal my own character, that it is charitable to all the virtuous men who aspire to noble and grand deeds".[5] There are a few passages which test this claim and shed light upon his character. He was not arrogant, but rather an unobtrusive man; prefaces, he says at the opening of his history,[6] are distasteful to him, being more often than not an excuse for the glorification of self and slandering others. He had a great admiration for Rome, which we must admit, in spite of Rome's faults, was justified. He seems to have believed in the *Fortuna Romae*,[7] which Augustus was doing so much to foster at that time; hence his consideration of the divine origin of Rome from Romulus and Remus. He preferred Roman mythology to that of the Greeks.[8]

Opinions of his value as a writer differ ("the less said about the *Roman Antiquities* the better", says one writer[9]). He assumes "that the first object of history is to please or to instruct rather than to tell the truth". Dionysius himself says that his history was not written for the sake of flattery;[10] he criticizes historians who disparage style;[11] he quotes his

[1] Ibid.   [2] I. 81.   [3] I. 7.
[4] I. 6. 5.   [5] I. 6. 5.   [6] I. 1.
[7] Cf. V. 7, 54: VII. 12: IX. 60. 1–7.   [8] II. 20 ff.
[9] F. A. Wright, *History of Later Greek Literature*, p. 185.
[10] I. 6. 5.   [11] I. 7. 1.

authorities,[1] forms his own opinion and gives reasons;[2] he cites as evidence written documents, altars, temples, and inscriptions;[3] he shows care in reading others' works.[4] "It is necessary", he says,[5] "to recount not only the military successes but to estimate the lives of generals", and "to understand the causes of wars".[6] The man who sets out primarily to "please or to instruct" would not take his history-writing thus seriously. It does not seem fair to say that Dionysius sought the truth as a secondary object: he tells aetiological myths, e.g. of Latinus, we admit, but most historians of the time would have done so when dealing with that period. Modern methods of historical criticism are not those of the early Empire, and are not a fair standard of judgement.

It is in some respects unfortunate that Dionysius the historian was also a rhetorician, because men illogically expect perfection in style from those who profess the art of style. So, looking at his style in the *Antiquities*, and finding it not entirely without blemish, many disparaged Dionysius. He at least stood for a purer style, the movement towards the Attic revival, as against the florid, turgid Asiatic style so prevalent in his day.[7] Yet Dionysius is ever a rhetorician: he is not a genius like Thucydides. A born writer needs to study style as Dionysius had certainly done; but to be a great historian, a rhetorician has to be a born writer as well. This is not disparaging Dionysius: he was no extraordinary man, but one of the more usual mediocrities. We must admire him for mastering the rules of style, and trying to apply them practically, in spite of the fact that he was not a born writer, that comparatively rare phenomenon.

2. *Style of Dionysius of Halicarnassus*

(*a*) A number of *poetical* words and phrases are to be found, such as νᾶμα, βρέτας, σκόπελος, ἐκπαγλέομαι, λιβάς, αὖλαξ,

---

[1] E.g. XIX. 3.   [2] I. 30.   [3] I. 53.
[4] I. 89. 4.   [5] V. 49.   [6] V. 56: X. 81: XI. 1. 2.
[7] Gilbert Murray, *Ancient Greek Literature*, p. 321.

παλίγκοτος, μελανείμων, ὄγκος, ἀσπαστός, ἀμείλικτος, ἄτεγκτος, ἐπιρροθέω, βέβηλος, δρόμος, φόβη, φρυκτωρία, θωπεύω, γεγωνός, ναματιαῖος—to mention only a few. In II. 38 we find the identical phrase of Aesch. *Ag.* 571 in παλίγκοτος τύχη.

(*b*) ἅπαξ λεγόμενα, *and rare and late words and phrases.* For example, ψαλιδωτός only in I. 68. 3; ἰσοκόρυφος only in III. 9. 7; ἐξαμάττω only in VI. 81. 4 in the metaphorical sense; πλήμμυρα (I. 7. 3) is found elsewhere only in Plutarch and the Anthologia Palatina; ἀλληλοκτόνος (I. 65. 5); ἀλληλοκτονιά (I. 87) elsewhere only in Moschio ap. Stobaeum, and Philo; τιθασός (I. 84. 1) is likewise rare and poetical. Of late words, we may take as examples καταστερίζω (I. 61) found in Diodorus and Plutarch, κλισιάδες (I. 66. 3 and V. 39) in Plutarch and Philo, αὔτανδρος in Polybius and Apollonius Rhodius, ἀναξιοπαθέω (IV. 11. 1) in Strabo, ἀχθοφορέω (IV. 81. 2) in Polybius and Plutarch. Many of these are fresh compounds and combinations of Classical Greek words.

(*c*) *Abstract nouns,* instead of participles, e.g. I. 9. 4: φιλανθρώπῳ ὑποδοχῇ τῶν δεομένων οἰκησέως . . . καὶ πολιτείας μεταδόσει τοῖς . . . ἐν πολεμῷ κρατηθεῖσι, δούλων . . . συγχωρήσει ἀστοῖς εἶναι, τύχης τε οὐδεμίας ἀπαξιώσει. Also XI. 59. 5: τὴν ἀναβολὴν τῆς περὶ αὐτοῦ διαγνώσεως . . . ἀκούσαντες. So too X. 10. 5: ἐπὶ φόνοις τῶν πολιτῶν καὶ διαστάσει τῆς πόλεως.

(*d*) *Thucydidean reminiscences.* ἀπαλλάττεσθαι occurs no less than seven times: the characteristic abstract noun with ποιεῖσθαι as an alternative to the equivalent verb is also common, e.g. ἐπίθεσιν ποιεῖσθαι (I. 84. 8; V. 7. 1); φυλακὴν ποιεῖσθαι (II. 13. 1), for φυλάττειν. A preference is also shown for the Attic ττ, e.g. V. 62, ταράττοντες, though this is not always the case, as shown by πράσσοντες in X. 55. 1.

(*e*) There is also frequently found *the use of* καὶ οὐ, καὶ οὔτε, καὶ μή, καὶ μηδείς, where the classical Greek would have been οὐ, οὔτε, μή, μηδείς.

(*f*) *Introductory particles* are sometimes omitted entirely, or only inadequate connecting particles are inserted, thus making the style rather rough and disconnected. The history starts abruptly thus, for example: τοὺς εἰωθότας ἀποδίδοσθαι . . .

(g) There is frequently found in Dionysius the use of *participles* in the same sentence, with an unexpected and unnecessary change of tense. E.g. I. 9. 3—καὶ διέμειναν . . . οὐκέτι πρὸς ἑτέρων ἐξελαθέντες . . . ὀνομάτων ἀλλαγαῖς διτταῖς . . . προσαγορευόμενοι . . . ὀνομασίαν ἔτι σώζοντες . . . Λατῖνοι ἀρξάμενοι καλεῖσθαι.

I. 78. 1—ἔρευναν ἐποιεῖτο . . . εἰσπέμπων καὶ . . . ἀπολιπών.

IV. 9. 1—με παραλαβὼν ἐξέθρεψεν οὐδὲν ἐνδεέστερον ἄγων τῶν ἑαυτοῦ τέκνων.

IV. 85. 1—οὐδενὶ τῶν ἄλλων φράσας ἠπείγετο τοὺς υἱοὺς παραλαβὼν καὶ τῶν ἑταίρων τοὺς πιστοτάτους, ἐλαύνων τοὺς ἵππους ἀπὸ ῥυτῆρος, ὡς φθάσων τὴν ἀπόστασιν.

V. 14. 1—διαπραξάμενοι ταῦτα . . . καὶ εὐτρεπισάμενοι . . . συνεῖχον . . . πυνθανόμενοι.

IX. 9. 9—ἐγκλινάντων δὲ καὶ φευγόντων.

X. 7. 3—προσδραμὼν, παίων καὶ λακτίζων καὶ πᾶσαν ἄλλην ὠμότητα καὶ ὕβριν ἐνδεικνύμενος.

X. 8. 4—τὰ χρήματα ἀποδοὺς . . . χωρίον ἐν ἑαυτῷ μικρὸν ὑπολειπόμενος.

XI. 5. 1—θορύβου δὲ πολλοῦ κατασχόντος τὸ συνέδριον καὶ τῶν μὲν πλείστων ἀγανακτούντων, ἀνίσταται . . .

The participles frequently are not neatly subordinated, and inadequately linked up. E.g. I. 41. 2—ἄγων κεχειρωμένος:

VI. 9. 5—ἵτε λαβόντες καλὰς ἐλπίδας ὡς ἕξοντες. . . ἐλευθερώσοντες . . . ἀποδώσοντες, οὐ περιοψόμενοι, γηραίως τε παρασκευάσοντες.

VI. 81. 2—ὃς δὶς ἀποδειχθεὶς ὕπατος δυναστείᾳ τῇ καλουμένῃ δικτατορίᾳ κράτιστα πάντων χρησάμενος . . . ἐποίησε . . .

VI. 92. 2—ἀκούσας δ' ὅτι . . ., μερίσας τὸν ἑαυτοῦ στρατὸν . . . τειχομαχεῖν ἔγνω Τῖτον Λάρκιον ἐπ' αὐτοῦ καταλιπών.

IX. 64. 3—οὓς ἰδόντες . . . ἀνέστρεφον ἀφέντες τὴν πολιορκίαν ἀτελῆ.

XI. 62. 4—ἀποτιθέμενοι τὰ περὶ τῆς χώρας ἐγκλήματα παρακαλοῦντες φίλοι γενέσθαι.

Such in brief outline are the main characteristics of Dionysius' style.

3. Dependence of Josephus on Dionysius of Halicarnassus

Although Josephus does not mention any dependence on Dionysius, it is clear that the title *Jewish Antiquities* was copied from the *Roman Antiquities*, and it may be that Dionysius' work inspired Josephus at the outset to write the history of his own nation in the same way. The division into twenty books is likewise copied by Josephus; the division being a deliberate one by the authors, and not arbitrarily imposed later for the convenience of copyists, as with Herodotus' history.

Given this dependence then, does a consideration of Josephus' *Jewish Antiquities* show traces of copying in detail, in words and phrases? Josephus' style when considered reveals much the same general characteristics as that of Dionysius, but for deciding on the actual dependence of Josephus on Dionysius, particular words and phrases are the best evidence, because some of the general points of style common to both were, to judge from other writers, becoming prevalent in Greek, and so the similarity of general characteristics does not necessarily indicate dependence. Any plausibility of the theory of the use of "assistants"[1] in *Antiquities* XVII–XIX (with still less probability, however, in XV and XVI) would mean that XVII–XIX cannot be cited as evidence either for or against dependence on Dionysius.

Particular instances of dependence may be tabulated thus:

Jos. *Ant.*	Dion. Hal. *Rom. Ant.*
VII. 220. ὑπόνομος	X. 53. 3.
XI. 177. θυρέος	II. 70. 3: IX. 64. 3.
XII. 8, 13 δραστήριος	III. 1. 3: IV. 4. 1: VIII. 13. 3, 14. 3. etc.

[1] *Contra Ap.* I. 50.

Jos. *Ant.*	Dion. Hal. *Rom. Ant.*
25. ὑποτυγχάνω (reply)	VI. 8. 7: VII. 16.
42. κατασκεύασμα	III. 2. 7.
76. καινουργέω	XI. 21.
81. τρανοτέρας	De Comp. 22
128. μετριοπαθέω	VIII. 61.
170. λιτότης	VI. 96. 2.
179. παρευδοκιμέω	De Vett. Cens. 3. 1.
230. εὔριπος	III. 68.
262. καταχωρίζω	I. 6 : V. 7. 2.
269. εὐαρέστησις	X. 57
305. παρεμβολή	III. 65. 5 : III. 61. 1.
315 etc.—e.g. XI. 161 : XIV. 427: XIX. 199— ἀπόγνωσις	I. 81; 87. 3 : III. 5. 2. IX. 12. 5.
334. ἀποσκευή	I. 52.
389. εὔκαιρος	De Dinarch. 7
430. κατάκοπος	VI. 29.
XIII. 31. ἀποσκήπτω	VI. 55.
129. μειόω	IV. 16; V. 2. 1; 13. 1. De Comp. 11.
152. γνωσιμαχέω	IX. 1.
189. φιλοφρόνησις cf. XIX. 318	X. 57.
358. προνομεύω	VIII. 11.
B.J. proem. εἰκαῖος	II. 64. 5.
II. 169. σημαία	VIII. 88. 1.
VII. 290. στρῶσις	III. 67. 5.
Life 116. πλεονέκτημα	cf. similar nouns in Dion. Hal. ῥᾳδιούργημα, λειτούργημα
πρόνοια *passim*	III. 4. 2.
XIV. 8. στασιαστής	VI. 70.
21. ἄζυξ	I. 40. 2; 40. 3.
43. πειρατήριον	VII. 37.
231. στρατολογία	VI. 44.
275. (*B.J.* III. 293)— αὔτανδρος	II. 6. 4.
296. ῥαΐζω	IV. 5. 2.
487. περιτροπή	V. 2.
XV. 44. (cf. XV. 37) ἀναξιοπαθέω	IV. 11. 1.

Jos. *Ant.*	Dion. Hal. *Rom. Ant.*
211, 388 (cf. XIX. 250)	
—ἀδημονέω	I. 56. 5 : III. 70. 3: V. 9. 3.
XVI. 93. ἐντήκω	VI. 72.
114. κενοσπουδέω	κενοσπουδία VI. 70
184. ἀντικατασκευάζω	I. 1.
201. προσκρούμα	IV. 23 : VII. 45 : X. 31.
267. μελανείμων	II. 19. 2. (Aesch. *Eum.* 376).
319. ἐνδοιασίμως	ἐνδοιάζω IV. 71. 1, 58 : VII. 59.
XIX. 184. ἐπαναρριπίζω	I. 59. 4 : VII. 15.
309. δράσσομαι cf. XIV.	
425. XV. 86. XVI. 216	IX. 21. 4.
318. ὑποκατακλίνομαι	VI. 24. 3, 61. 2.
(cf. XII. 21)	
XX. 53. ἀοίδιμος	II. 66. 4.

It is characteristic of Dionysius that he does not force his opinion on his readers, but gives them the evidence on both sides: if puzzled and unable to judge either way, he frankly says so (e.g. I. 56; II. 32. 1; IX. 18), but when both views seem equally plausible he gives his own interpretation, leaving the reader to judge for himself from the data which he has given. There is thus, as Thackeray points out,[1] a frequently recurring phrase which he uses in such cases, e.g. I. 48. 1— κρινέτω δ᾽ ὡς ἕκαστος τῶν ἀκουόντων βούλεται. Sometimes it is expanded or modified, but the main outline is the same, e.g. I. 48. 4—ἐχέτω δ᾽ ὅπῃ τις αὐτὸν πείθει: II. 40. 30—ἀλλ᾽ ὑπὲρ μὲν τούτων κρινέτω τις ὡς βούλεται: II. 70. 5—εἰ δὲ ὀρθῶς ὑπείληφα . . . ὁ βουλόμενος συμβαλεῖ: III. 35. 6—κρινέτω δ᾽ ἕκαστος ὡς βούλεται. In these contexts he is dealing with apparently supernatural events. The same characteristic is found in Josephus, e.g. I. 108—περὶ μὲν οὖν τούτων, ὡς ἂν ἑκάστοις ᾖ φίλον, οὕτω σκοπείτωσαν, where the context, like that of the examples in Dionysius, deals with miraculous events (e.g. in I. 108 with reference to the long life of the patriarchs). So too in II. 349—περὶ μὲν οὖν τούτων ὡς ἑκάστῳ δοκεῖ διαλαμβανέτω: III. 81—καὶ περὶ μὲν οὖν τούτων ὡς βούλεται

---

[1] *Josephus the Man and the Historian*, p. 57.

φρονείτω ἕκαστος τῶν ἐντευξομένων: III. 269: III. 322: IV. 159: VIII. 262: XIX. 108: X. 281 (a longer form): XVII. 354—ὅτῳ δ᾽ ἀπιστεῖται τὰ τοιάδε, γνώμης ὀνινάμενος τῆς ἑαυτοῦ κώλυμα οὐκ ἂν γένοιτο τῷ ἐπ᾽ ἀρετὴν αὐτὰ προστιθεμένῳ: B.J. V. 257. This is important evidence that Josephus copied Dionysius' language and style.

Dionysius uses ἴδιος in place of the reflexive pronoun for variety, e.g. II. 76. 1: III. 22. 5: IV. 4. 4. The same characteristic is found in Josephus, e.g. Ant. XII. 281, 285, who also uses οἰκεῖος for further variety, e.g. XII. 423: XIII. 84, 202: XV. 159, 218, 239, 264, 288, 330: XVI. 27, 37, 60, 138, 147, 276, 277. The construction διὰ [τινὸς] ἔχειν, ποιεῖν, εἶναι, γίγνεσθαι is very common in both writers, e.g. Dion. Hal. III. 22. 1—δι᾽ αἰτίας ἔχειν: VII. 62. 3—δι᾽ ἁρπαγῆς. Josephus has all the varieties of the construction, and in addition a modified form ἐν [τινὶ] ἔχειν etc., e.g. XII. 60—δι᾽ ἀσφελείας ἔχειν: XIII. 273—ἐν ἀποδόσει ἔχειν: XIV. 298—διὰ φρουρᾶς ἔχειν: XV. 195—διὰ πάσης τιμῆς: XVI. 214—διὰ σπουδῆς εἶναι: XVII. 106—δι᾽ οἴκτου καταστῆναι: XVIII. 72. 196, 325—διὰ λόγων ἐλθεῖν: XIX. 274—δι᾽ ἐγκωμίων ἄγειν: Life 414—διὰ τιμῆς ἄγειν. It is noticeable too that when there are two forms of a verb's tenses or a noun's conjugation, Dionysius and Josephus frequently have the same form, e.g. ἐφθάσθην, Jos. Ant. VIII. 307, Dion. Hal. VI. 25. 3; ἀγήοχα, Jos. Ant. XIV. 394, XV. 383, Dion. Hal. X. 6. Sometimes Josephus uses two different forms, e.g. οἴδασι, B.J. II. 91, III. 363: and ἴσασι, Ant. XIV. 3, XVI. 45. (συνοίδασι, occurs in Dionysius IV. 36, and VI. 47. 2; though he more regularly uses ἴσασι.) With the forms βασιλεῖς, βασιλέας, for example, some Josephus manuscripts have one form, some another, e.g. βοῦς (Jos. Ant. XVII. 347), cf. Dion. Hal. I. 39 (passim.) Josephus is fond of compound verbs with two prepositions affixed, e.g. ὑποκατασκευάζω (XV. 97); ἀντιμεταλαμβάνω (XVI. 66); ἐπιδιαλλάττω (XVI. 175, cf. XVII. 376); ἀντιμεταχωρέω (XV. 16); ἀντιπαραδίδωμι (XV. 41); ἀντιμετασπάω (XIII. 143); and compounds of words common in classical Greek uncompounded, e.g. καιροφυλακέω (XVI. 84). Compare from Dionysius ἀντιμετατάσσω (Dion. Hal. III. 3. 25, cf. *De Thuc.* 91); φιλεργέω (V. 66. 2); ἡ δεκαετία (I. 75. 3); ἰδιόζενος (I. 84.3); ἀλληλοκτονέω (I. 65) (ἀλληλοκτονία I. 87. 3); κτηνοφορέω (II. 9. 1); ἀχθοφορέω (IV. 81. 2); θυμομαχέω (V. 11. 2). Thus, the usage, if not the actual words, may have been copied from Dionysius by Josephus.

Taken altogether then, the examples show that the influence of Dionysius on the style of Josephus is considerable, and that it amounts to deliberate imitation in some cases. It is curious, however, that Josephus does not so much as mention Dionysius to whom he owes so much in many ways. Judging by present-day standards, we should expect such dependence to be noted, and at such an omission we should look askance. But it was quite in accordance with the custom of the time of Josephus not to make any such mention. The same is the case with the use of authorities among the ancients: frequently authorities are extensively used (e.g. Josephus and the *Letter of Aristeas—Ant.* XII. 11–118), without any mention. It is not that the feeling of gratitude was not experienced in those days, but only that the modern ideas of reservation of copyright were not formulated, let alone enforced.

NOTE

The " historical" and " rhetorical" styles. There is an important distinction between these two styles: the "historical" aims primarily at narrating events plainly and simply (cf. the "narrative" passages in Thucydides): the "rhetorical" aims at presenting a more elaborate narrative. The genius of a true historian is needed to produce either style correctly: if care is not taken, the "historical" style may lead to the fault of an over-emphasis upon the facts as distinct from the way in which they are presented (as with Polybius), and the "rhetorical" style may lead to a highly coloured narrative, with the presentation of the facts as an entirely secondary consideration.

C. Josephus and Polybius

The references to Polybius in Josephus' works are as follows:

Ant. XII. 135 f. Josephus quotes the eleventh book of the histories of Polybius—"Scopas the general of Ptolemaeus set out for the Upper regions, and reduced the Jewish nation in the winter": he also quotes Polybius (*Ant.* XII. 136) for the statement that, after the defeat of Scopas by Antiochus, "Antiochus took over Batanea, and Samaria, and Abila and Gadara, but after a short time those of the Jews also who dwell around the temple called Jerusalem came over to him."

Ant. XII. 358, 359. Josephus disagrees with Polybius' statement that the spoiling of the Temple of Artemis was the occasion of the death of Antiochus, but believes rather that it was the spoiling of the Temple at Jerusalem.

Contra Apionem II. 84 (the Latin version alone is here extant). Polybius is cited, along with Strabo, Nicolaus of Damascus, Timagenes, Castor, and Apollodorus, in support of the view that Antiochus "pecuniis indigentem transgressum foedera Judaeorum et spoliasse templum auro argentoque plenum".

It is certain then that Josephus consulted Polybius' history, but it is only used as a secondary source. The main source, though unnamed, for *Ant.* XII. 240–XIII. 212 is 1 Maccabees, and in XII. 358 f Polybius is only cited because Josephus is at pains to disagree with his statement. Again, between *Ant.* XII. 118, where Josephus' source, the *Letter of Aristeas*, ends, and *Ant.* XII. 240, where his next source, 1 Maccabees, begins, Polybius is quoted (*Ant.* XII. 135, 136). This further shows the use Josephus made of Polybius as a secondary source, to fill in the gap between his two main sources. As Strabo is used in a similar way between the end of 1 Maccabees (*Ant.* XIII. 212) and *Ant.* XV, at which point Josephus is well on his way with the particularly detailed narrative of the rise of Herod and his subsequent reign (using Nicolaus of Damascus as his main source), so Polybius seems to be used between the end of *Aristeas* and the beginning of 1 Maccabees. In *Contra Apionem* II. 84 Polybius is cited along with others in confirmation of a statement, and there is no question of his having been used as a primary source in this work, but only as secondary.

Polybius of Megalopolis was born about 208 B.C., and died about 127 B.C. His father was Lycortas, a prominent statesman of the Achaean League. At the age of nineteen Polybius seems to have taken part in a Roman expedition against the "Celts" (189 B.C.). On the disruption of the Achaean League, which followed the defeat of Perseus at Pydna in 168 by L. Aemilius Paullus, Polybius was taken as a hostage to Rome. He remained there for seventeen years, when he was allowed to return, with the other hostages. He became a member of the Scipionic Circle while in Rome.

The history which Polybius wrote was in forty books, of which the first five are preserved complete. It dealt with the period from the First Punic War (264 B.C.) to the destruction of Carthage and Corinth (146 B.C.), and included the fortunes of Asia, Syria, Egypt, Carthage, Macedonia, and Greece.

A certain parallel with Josephus is immediately to be recognized. Both historians left their homes for Rome, but whereas Polybius returned to his fatherland, Josephus did not. Both became mediators for their countrymen with the Romans. Both were intimate with the leading men of their day, Polybius with the Scipionic Circle, Josephus with Vespasian, Titus, and Agrippa II.[1] But Josephus was looked upon as a traitor by the Jews, while Polybius on his return was honoured by statues in some Peloponnesian towns. Both wrote histories dealing partly with events through which they themselves had lived. There is a certain similarity of views too. Polybius, no doubt inspired by the Scipionic Circle, saw a certain completeness and unity in the apparently isolated

[1] Agrippa II and Titus were bound together by the affection of Titus for Berenice.

8—S.I.J.

conquests of the Romans, and had a great admiration for the
Roman Republic, which he thought was supreme in the realm
of politics, but inferior to Greece in the realm of intellect.
Josephus too had great admiration of the qualities of the
Romans, and of their irresistible strength, and to show this
was his purpose in writing the *Jewish War*.

Dependence upon Polybius by Josephus as a secondary
source has been shown, and the parallel between the two is so
close that dependence for style also is *a priori* reasonable.
Looking at the style of Polybius, it can be seen that the
characteristics to be found in Josephus are, for the most part,
to be paralleled in Polybius.

(*a*) Compared with Josephus, Polybius seems to make a
fuller use of connecting particles, whereas Josephus frequently
omits them, or does not use them adequately. Polybius rarely
omits them, and has a greater variety, correctly used. In Book
III, for example, Polybius entirely omits a connecting particle
twenty-two times, eleven of which examples occur in decrees
or speeches: τε is used alone four times only, and οὖν alone
ten times.

(*b*) Involution. E.g. Polyb. II. 1. 1—τοῖς ἐκτὸς ἐγχειρεῖν
ἤρξαντο πράγμασιν.

(*c*) Perfect and Pluperfect Tenses for classical Aorist. E.g.
Polyb. I. 4. 7—γεγονότες: II. 12. 4—ἐπεποίηντο.

(*d*) The Thucydidean ποιεῖσθαι + abstract noun. E.g.,
Polyb. II. 2. 1—τὴν πρώτην διάβασιν ποιεῖσθαι. σφεῖς and
σφέτερος are used, e.g. Polyb. IV. 9. 2.

(*e*) The forms γίνεσθαι for γίγνεσθαι, γινώσκειν for γιγνώσκειν:
γίνεσθαι e.g. Polyb. I. 2. 6: γινώσκειν, e.g. Polyb. I. 3. 4.

(*f*) A more abstract mode of expression instead of the
highly idiomatic concrete use. E.g. Polyb. IV. 9. 5—χωρὶς
τῆς τῶν Ἀχαιῶν βουλήσεως: IV. 11. 4—διὰ τὴν ἐπίφασιν τῆς
ἑτοιμότητος τῶν Ἀχαιῶν.

(*g*) Use of participles:

(i) In Genitive Absolute constructions "hanging" at the
end of a sentence. E.g. Polyb. I. 78. 11—ἐνίκων . . . , καλῶς

μὲν θηρίων ἀγωνισαμένων, ἐπιφανεστάτην δὲ τοῦ Ναραύα
παρασχομένου χρείαν.

(ii) With tenses not strictly subordinated to the main verb.
E.g. Polyb. IV. 75. 3—ἀκούων δ' . . . καὶ κρίνας . . . προκα-
τελάβετο.

(h) Characteristic compounds. E.g. Polyb. IV. 63. 10—
σιτομετρέω: 46. 1—φιλοχωρέω: 36. 4—ἀντοφθαλμέω: 32. 7—
ἀχθοφορέω: 82. 3—κακοπραγμονέω: 10. 9—φυγομαχέω: III.
49. 11—καινοποιέω: 70. 4—καινοτομέω.

Taking separate words and phrases, we can exclude all
technical military words, because by Josephus' time, these,
though coming from Polybius perhaps in the first place, had
become stereotyped and common. Other words found in both
authors are: ἀσμενίζω (Ant. XIII. 413; Polyb. VI. 8. 3);
ἀκέραιος (Ant. XII. 37; Polyb. I. 45. 2, etc.); αὔτανδρος
(Ant. XIV. 275; Polyb. I. 23. 7); δικαιολογέομαι (Ant. XIV.
50; Polyb. IV. 3. 12); δυσέντευκτος (Ant. XIII. 35; Polyb.
V. 34. 4); ἐπιβάθρα (Ant. XI. 307; Polyb. III. 24. 14);
ἐπιστροφή (Ant. XII. 149; Polyb. 4. 4. 4); εὔκαιρος (Ant. XII.
389; Polyb. IV. 38, etc.); κατασκεύασμα (Ant. XII. 42;
Polyb. IV. 18. 8: X. 27. 9); καταστροφή (Ant. XII. 300;
Polyb. V. 54. 4, etc.); μισοπονηρέω (Ant. XIII. 275 (+Dat.);
Polyb. IX. 39. 6); προγονικός (Ant. XII. 146; Polyb. III. 64);
σωρεύω (Ant. XII. 211; Polyb. XVI. 11. 4); σωρηδόν (Ant.
XIV. 460; Polyb. I. 34. 5); φιλοζωέω (Ant. XII. 301;
Polyb. XI. 2. 11).

But though the same word occurs in both authors, it is
often used with a difference by extension, e.g. ἀσμενίζω with
a participle, as in Ant. XIII. 413, is not in Polybius, who
uses the word with accusative, dative, and ἐπί with dative;
similarly μισοπονηρεῖν τοῖς Σαμαρεῦσιν (Ant. XIII. 275) is an
extension of the Polybian usage: Josephus has στρατεύσιμος
ἡλικία (Ant. XII. 366); Polybius has οἱ στρατεύσιμοι (VI. 19. 6).
τὸ δυσέντευκτον in Ant. XIII. 35 is hardly the same as in
Polybius V. 34. 4, where Ptolemy Philopator is described as

δυσέντευκτος and ἀνεπίστατος. ἐπιβάθρα in *Ant.* XI. 307 is metaphorical, while in Polybius III. 24. 14 the word is used literally. It may therefore be said that the conscious imitation of Polybian vocabulary is slight. The general stylistic characteristics found in Polybius, though found in Josephus, are not exclusive to the former and can be paralleled in Dionysius of Halicarnassus and Nicolaus of Damascus; so that Josephus' style in all probability rather represents that of the age in which he was writing, the age of the Κοινή Greek.

Polybius then is used as a secondary source, and though there may be a little imitation of Polybius, whom Josephus would certainly have included in his wide reading of Greek literature, it is more than counter-balanced by the imitation of Dionysius of Halicarnassus, with whom Josephus has a closer affinity than with Polybius of Megalopolis.

D. JOSEPHUS AND STRABO

Disproportion in the *Jewish Antiquities* is partly due to Josephus' sources; where they are full, his narrative is full, and where they are lacking, his narrative becomes incomplete. The period of almost four hundred years from the Return to the reign of Antiochus Epiphanes is contained in two books (*Ant.* XI, XII) but the reign of Herod the Great (37–4 B.C.), and his rise to fame, are dealt with in over three books (XIV, XV, XVI, and part of XVII). For *Ant.* XI and XII the underlying sources are the Greek Esdras A (*Ant.* XI. 1—c. 156), Nehemiah (*Ant.* XI. 159–c. 180), Esther (*Ant.* XI. 186–c. 296), an account of Alexander the Great (cf. especially *Ant.* XI. 313–347), the so-called *Letter of Aristeas* (*Ant.* XII. 11–118), and 1 Maccabees (*Ant.* XII. 240–XIII. 212).

After this point,[1] at which the death of Jonathan is reached, there are no more specifically Jewish works known to us which Josephus could have used as his sources. But, very conveniently, the *Jewish War* is used as a source from the

---

[1] *Ant.* XIII. 212.

point where 1 Maccabees finishes (*Ant.* XIII. 212). In their editions, both Naber and Niese add a footnote at *Ant.* XIII. 215, comparing *B.J.* I. 50 (I. 2. 2.). Until Josephus reached the rise of Herod, he seems to have been in difficulty about sources, e.g. in *Ant.* XIV. 190–264, where the long list of decrees is not entirely relevant.[1]

One of the intermediate sources thus used between the end of 1 Maccabees, and the rise of Herod (at which point he is mainly dependent upon Nicolaus of Damascus), is Strabo. The references to him are as follows:

Ant. XIII. 285–7. In 285, Cleopatra's quarrel with Ptolemy Lathyrus, and her appointment of Chelcias and Ananias as generals, are mentioned. Strabo is cited to confirm this (286), and his actual words are quoted (287).

Ant. XIII. 319. Dealing with the death of Aristobulus, Josephus describes his character, and quotes Strabo "on the authority of Timagenes" in confirmation.

Ant. XIII. 347. Strabo and Nicolaus are cited testifying to the fact that Ptolemy bade his soldiers murder Jews and put their bodies into "boiling caldrons".

Ant. XIV. 35. Josephus mentions the gift of Aristobulus to Pompey on his arrival at Damascus, and quotes Strabo's account of it. There is doubt about the length of the citation from Strabo.[2] Naber ends it at δημιούργημα (35), Niese at ταλάντων (36).

Ant. XIV. 68. Strabo's name is coupled with those of Nicolaus and Livy, to prove that, during Pompey's capture of Jerusalem (63 B.C.), the priests stood fast at the altars.

Ant. XIV. 111. Crassus' action in taking the Temple treasures is the occasion of a slight digression. Strabo is quoted as saying (112) that Mithridates took from Cos eight hundred talents belonging to the Jews. In 115–18, Strabo

[1] Cf. Karl Albert. *Strabo als Quelle des Flavius Josephus*, Aschaffenburg 1902.
[2] It is important to note that *if* the quotation ends at δημιούργημα, and not at δυνάστην (Shillito), then Josephus has verified a historical statement.

is further quoted as saying that the Jews during Sulla's war with Mithridates formed one quarter of the population of Cyrene; that they have penetrated the whole "inhabited world", including Egypt, where, at Alexandria, they have an "ethnarch", specially appointed.

Ant. XIV. 138. Strabo is cited as an authority to support the statement that Hyrcanus joined in an expedition to Egypt. Strabo, says Josephus, is quoting "Asinius" (Pollio) in one place, and on another occasion "Hypsicrates".

Ant. XV. 9. The actual words of Strabo are given here, showing that Antony put Antigonus to death by beheading him.

All the references to Strabo, then, are confined to three books, *Ant.* XIII–XV. We may say then that Strabo is a subsidiary source, used to fill in a gap, and to supplement the meagre sources which Josephus had between the end of 1 Maccabees (*Ant.* XIII. 212) and *Ant.* XV, at which point Josephus is well occupied with the very full narrative of the rise of Herod, and his reign.[1]

Strabo's work was suited for use as a subsidiary source. Born at Amasia in Pontus before 50 B.C.,[2] of wealthy parents, he visited Rome frequently on his extensive travels. He died after A.D. 21.[3] He wrote a *Geography*, which has survived, in 17 books. Like Polybius, he admired Rome greatly, and wrote a history in 47 books, of which only fragments survive. This was intended as a supplement to that of Polybius. It recounted events prior to the commencement of Polybius' history in 264 B.C., and later than the end of his history in 146 B.C.

---

[1] Ending, with Herod's death, at *Ant.* XVII. 191.

[2] Meyer (Paul) *Quaestiones Strabonianae*, Leipzig 1879, says Strabo's birth was "ante annum 54 ante Christum n.": 64–63 B.C. is given in the Introduction to the Loeb Strabo.

[3] A.D. 21 (according to the Introduction to the Loeb Strabo) is the date of the death of Juba II which Strabo mentions. The date is not certain but it is known that Ptolemaeus was on the throne in A.D. 23 (*Camb. Anc. Hist.* X. p. 644; Tac. *Annals* IV. 5. 3—Furneaux, note ad loc.).

and went down as far as the Imperial era.[1] His work was of an encyclopaedic nature, comparable, in this respect, with the *Universal History* of Nicolaus in 144 books, and would for this reason be a useful standby for historians like Josephus when they had any gaps to fill.

[1] As he inserts in the *Geography* a reference to the death of Juba (XVII. 7), he may have brought his *History* also up to date.

CHAPTER 6

THE EDITIONS AND TEXTS OF JOSEPHUS' WORKS

THE first printed edition of the works of Josephus was published in 1470; it contained the Latin version of the *Jewish Antiquities*. There followed editions likewise of the Latin version, published in Venice in 1486[1] and 1499, containing the *Antiquities*, the *Jewish War*, and the *Contra Apionem*. According to Fabricius,[2] this was thought by Gesner, wrongly, to have been the first edition; it was, however, the first *complete* edition of the Latin version. Next, there was an edition by Goullet from Paris in 1513. In 1524 an edition was published in Basel by Frobenius, "the most polished and best of all",[3] according to Niese: care was shown in its compilation and the treatment of the manuscripts, made more accessible by the previous editions mentioned. Another edition was produced in Basel in 1534 by Gelenius:[4] Niese says[5] that this was produced by Frobenius, with the comment that this edition and the rest of the editions of Josephus in Latin were not trustworthy, since the Latin is emended from the Greek. This seems to be an overstatement. Frobenius' second edition was published in Basel beginning in 1548, four years after the first Greek edition in 1544. It is therefore hardly true to say, with Niese, that after 1544 and the publication of a Greek edition,

---

[1] Niese, vol. I, praefatio, p. lxx mentions the 1470 edition, and then says, "secuta est alia edita Venetiis anno, si typothetae fides, 1400". This cannot be a correct date, nor can Niese have intended this, since he says *secuta* (i.e. after 1470).

[2] *De Josepho et eius Scriptis* in the "Introduction" to Hudson's edition.

[3] Niese, loc. cit.

[4] Ex emendatione Sigism. Gelenius, so Fabricius, ap. Hudson, loc. cit.

[5] See ref. in note 1.

"learned men did not pay attention to the Latin version". But it is true, nevertheless, that since 1544 there has been no complete major edition of the Latin version. Fabricius enumerates such efforts as were made until 1564 with the publication of the Latin version as such.

There was an edition published in Geneva in 1611, setting out the *Antiquities* and the *Life* in Greek with Gelenius'[1] version, the *Jewish War* and *Contra Apionem* with the version ascribed to Rufinus, and including the Book of the Maccabees together with Erasmus' paraphrase of it. This edition paid special attention to certain Greek manuscripts from the Palatine Library and was republished in 1635; a promised volume containing variant readings provided from these manuscripts did not appear. A further edition was published at Leipzig in 1691, which according to Fabricius followed closely the Geneva edition; the name "Coloniae" was given for its place of origin instead of Leipzig, and it was the work of Thomas Ittig. This was followed by Bernard's edition published at Oxford in 1700, which had the benefit of the unfinished work of others, and was itself uncompleted.

Nevertheless, the edition of Hudson[2] made use of the material included in Bernard's incomplete edition. Attention was paid to the variant readings of the manuscripts, and a Latin translation given in parallel columns to the Greek text. Hudson evidently devoted many years' work[3] to the preparation of his edition, and his task was heavy. But he finally avoided the pitfall into which Bernard had fallen with the collection of an unwieldy mass of material, by concentrating more upon giving the variant readings of the manuscripts rather than upon a mass of notes. This edition, with the care bestowed upon it and the manuscript information which it contains, is a landmark.

[1] Basel 1534, v. supra.
[2] 2 vols., Oxford 1720.
[3] See in Hudson's edition, vol. I, the Dedication, "Viro longe nobilissimo Jacobo Bruges . . ."

Havercamp's [1] edition followed in 1726, which made use of Bernard's notes, omitted for the most part by Hudson, included Hudson's notes and Latin version, and added further notes and conjectures by Cocceius, and Spanhemus especially, and the collations of the Paris manuscripts, including R and P, made by J. Philip of Orville. Havercamp's massive edition did not attempt to produce an improved text so much as to collect together results of work done on the manuscripts of Josephus.

There was a tendency to use Havercamp's edition rather than Hudson's in subsequent publications, as for example those of Ernesti,[2] Oberthür,[3] and Richter.[4] The last two editions were published with the aim of popularizing Josephus' works and making them available at a moderate price, and there was no attempt to incorporate deviations from Havercamp's edition.

Dindorf returned to a more critical attitude to the text in his edition of 1845–7,[5] as his Preface at the beginning of the second volume shows. Having praised Hudson for his critical work in his edition, Dindorf said that he nevertheless left by far the most of such work to be done by others, and that Havercamp's edition for all its influence and subsequent use did not carry on Hudson's intention. So Dindorf used Havercamp's *apparatus* to make a number of emendations to the text, and to remove some obvious corruptions by conjectures. He paid particular attention [6] to the Latin translation, which was printed parallel to the Greek text as in Hudson, and aimed to make the Latin translation to follow more closely the Greek than was the case in Hudson's edition. Dindorf's edition is therefore of special importance.

Dindorf referred [7] enthusiastically to Cardwell's edition [8] of the *Jewish War*, because Cardwell shared his aim of discovering from the comparison of the manuscript readings as far as

---

[1] 2 vols., Amsterdam, Leyden, Utrecht.   [2] Leipzig 1795.
[3] Leipzig, 3 vols., 1782–5.   [4] Leipzig, 6 vols., 1826–7.
[5] Paris, 2 vols.   [6] See Preface to vol. I.
[7] Preface, vol. 2.   [8] Oxford 1837, 2 vols.

possible the text which Josephus wrote. In Cardwell's own words:[1] "Conferendi sunt Codices, describendae lectionum varietates, adornandus ad eorum fidem textus, purganda vetus Rufini versio, instruenda notarum supellex." Accordingly, Cardwell collated six manuscripts of the *Jewish War*, concluding that the manuscript P was of especial importance for ascertaining the true text of Josephus' work. His Latin translation was printed separately in the second volume, not in parallel columns with the Greek, as in Hudson and Dindorf.

In a real sense, the editions of Cardwell and Dindorf are complimentary.

Bekker's edition [2] followed Dindorf, but both were satisfied with the *apparatus* given in Havercamp. Meanwhile, Holwerda in 1847 published emendations to the text of Josephus, accompanied by investigation into his language and style. This was an important development, and can be said to mark the era of the modern study of this author. A new edition was clearly required.

In 1873, Niese began work on his edition, spending two and a half years in libraries in Italy and Paris collating manuscripts; he claimed to have known and collated all Greek manuscripts of any importance.[3] His edition [4] is the fullest and most thorough which we possess. Where he gives a reading different from that of the manuscripts, the manuscript readings are given in the notes. His view was that the manuscripts RO provide the best readings, and he shows preference for this group. The work involved was prodigious, and Niese himself did not claim too much in the way of complete accuracy, being satisfied, if at least the groundwork had been covered, that others should continue the task.

Naber's edition followed.[5] In a sense this edition was a continuation of Niese's work, for as Niese pointed out, there was much which he had left undone, but Naber's edition is based

[1] Vol. I. p. vi.   [2] Leipzig 1855.
[3] Praef. vol. I. p. lxxv.   [4] Berlin 1887–95.
[5] 6 vols, Teubner edition 1888–96, Leipzig.

on some different views from those of Niese. Niese's preference for the manuscripts RO is to be contrasted with Naber's statement:[1] "Codex R perite tractatus saepe proderit, sed seatet vitiosis lectionibus et lacunis, quae sine reliquis libris sanari non possunt." On the whole, Naber prefers the manuscript M. It is clear from his Preface, that it is not a matter simply of deciding between two or more variant readings: there is also the important aspect of the language and style characteristic of Josephus. The latter will assist in the former, and both need to be taken into account. But the realization of the need to ascertain more about the language and style of Josephus leads to a complex problem, which perhaps Niese had not studied sufficiently, if for no other reason than that he carried out a vast amount of work upon the manuscripts. Naber's contribution to the study of Josephus is that he recognized this complex element; he had the benefit not only of Holwerda's notes and published work which were mentioned earlier, but also of Dindorf's conclusions on the matter. Niese said [2] simply that Dindorf aimed to "recall Josephus to the style of the Attic writers", and that a decision on this could not be made at that stage. Unfortunately a general view on the style of Josephus must be included or implied when a decision is made about his text. Naber, therefore, is right in saying [3] that Dindorf, and the work on the style of Josephus undertaken by him and Holwerda, is too much neglected by Niese.

The editions of Niese and Naber, therefore, both need to be considered for the information about manuscript readings which they contain, and for the assessment of their worth.

The Loeb edition of Josephus was begun [4] by the late Dr St J. Thackeray, who stated:[5] "Yet one may respectfully question whether he [Niese] has established a definitive text." Recognizing, as Thackeray did, the debt which is owed to Niese, it should be said that Niese did not establish a definitive text: Naber's work showed so much. Thackeray was careful

---

[1] Praef. vol. I. p. iv.   [2] Praef. p. lxxv.   [3] Praef. p. v.
[4] 1926–   .   [5] Intro. p. xvii.

to state that a reading was not to be adopted simply because it was supported by a particular group of manuscripts: "Each variant has to be considered on its merits."[1] On the whole, he preferred the manuscript combination PRA for the true text, thus avoiding Niese's emphasis on PRO, and Naber's on AMW.

Thackeray lived to complete the first four volumes of this edition, containing the *Life*, the *Contra Apionem*, the *Jewish War*, and the first four books of the *Jewish Antiquities*. When he died in 1930, he had already sent to press material for the fifth volume. His unfinished task was taken over by Dr Marcus, and with the publication of the seventh volume in 1943, the end of Book XIV of the *Antiquities* was reached. Marcus agrees with the view of Thackeray concerning the respective value of the manuscript groups in attempting to arrive at the text of Josephus, and claims that he based his text upon "a careful and independent study of the MS. evidence, with the result that it does not agree entirely with either Niese's or Naber's".[2] Two volumes have yet to be published to complete the Loeb edition, and will contain Books XV–XX of the *Jewish Antiquities*.

Upon the completion of this edition, it will be easier to assess the importance attached to the particular manuscripts or group of manuscripts, and especially to the Latin version. Manuscripts of this version are more plentiful, but there does not exist at present a work on them with special reference to the groups into which they fall, similar to the great work which Niese did on the Greek manuscripts.[3] This is the first outstanding point which emerges from this consideration of the texts and editions of Josephus so far published.

[1] Intro. p. xviii.
[2] Vol. VI. p. vi, Prefatory Note; cf. Thackeray, vol. II, p. xxvii: "careful and independent investigation of the MS. evidence."
[3] Niese referred (vol. V. Preface, p. vii) to the proposed complete edition by Boysen in the *Corpus Scriptorum Ecclesiasticorum Latinorum*, Vienna; Part 6 only has been issued.

The second is connected closely with the first. It is significant that Thackeray's study of Josephus led him to set about the compilation of a *Lexicon to Josephus*, of which the first part [1] was published before his death. Marcus took over the task of publication, and three more parts have appeared to date.[2] The *Lexicon*'s main function was to "elucidate the meaning of an important historian, with a very uneven style".[3] The unevenness of style has caused difficulties, especially with the text, because unless the unevenness is understood and allowed for, there may be a desire to "correct" it. Hence the close connection of the linguistic work on Josephus and the text. Thackeray's *Lexicon*, as he pointed out,[4] was not the first study of the style and grammar of Josephus, for Schmidt [5] did some pioneer work in this field. But the development and application of this work is likely to have important results, for, as has been suggested elsewhere,[6] the unevenness of Josephus' style is not necessarily to be explained or accounted for by adopting the view that he entrusted certain parts of, for example, the *Antiquities*, to a "Sophoclean" or "Thucydidean" assistant. The *Lexicon* is of great importance in this connection.

[1] A to ἀργός, Paris 1930.
[2] Part 2, 1934; Part 3, 1948; Part 4, 1955.
[3] Part 1, Preface, p. vii.
[4] Loc. cit.
[5] *De Flavii Josephi elocutione observationes criticae*, Leipzig 1893.
[6] Chap. IV.

CHAPTER 7

JOSEPHUS
The Man and the Historian

A MAN is not necessarily a historian, but a historian is inevitably a human being, that is, he possesses the attributes and the feelings which together constitute a man. It is therefore impossible to separate entirely the man and the historian, as if they were two distinct entities in one individual, because they are interconnected and mutually supplementary: any such distinction is made purely for the sake of convenience in forming an estimate of the author of a historical work, but there is a danger of assuming without justification that what is a matter of convenience is a matter of fact.

An estimate of any historian must rest upon the basic fact that the historian is a man, and therefore the "man" and the "historian" can only be fully comprehended in the light of each other. Whether this should be so ideally, is a question not within the present scope: the fact must be conceded.

A study of Josephus the man is thus one of the means of arriving at an estimate of Josephus the historian. It involves the two problems: "What is the most reasonable view to take of the character of Josephus, bearing in mind the numerous and diverse opinions which have been held of him?", and, "To what extent did his character influence his history?"

When Josephus was only fourteen years of age, "the chief-priests and prominent men in the city",[1] he says, used to consult him about the Law. He was then clever, and showed his talents early. As he became older, he still showed his ability.

[1] *Life* 9.

A man who was not clever and able could not have retained, let alone won, the honoured position which Josephus had at Rome, from the destruction of Jerusalem (A.D. 70) until his death (after A.D. 100). An ability to rise and fulfil positions of trust has been characteristic of other Jews throughout history; Josephus was in no respect an exception.

He had a taste for literature, which exhibited itself from youth.[1] The assiduous way in which he must have turned his attention to Greek classics in order to improve his style and knowledge of the language is characteristic.[2] Behind his thoroughness there must have been at least a little appreciation of the literature he was studying. He was practically efficient: his careful choice of a sect, before finally joining himself with the Pharisees,[3] the successful embassy on which he went to Rome,[4] and his defence of Jotapata (whatever view is taken of his motives), all go to confirm this.

Himself a priest, with royal Hasmonean blood in his veins, and conscious of his brilliance as a youth, he was tempted to let his ambition get the upper hand, and gave way to it. Hence, where his personal interests were at stake, he became unscrupulous, leading himself into inconsistencies. This seems to explain his career in Galilee. To say that the account in the *Jewish War*, that Josephus went as a "general",[5] is right as contrasted with the statement in the *Life* that he went as one of three "ambassadors", is doubtful, considering that the *Life* was occasioned by the *Jewish War* of his rival Justus, whose main purpose was to attack Josephus' conduct in Galilee. So Josephus covered up his restatement of his position with a counter-attack upon Justus. Events point to the theory that Josephus did act as "general" in Galilee, but acted *ultra vires*; he was sent on a mission of pacification, at least for the moment, with two others,[6] and emerged fighting the Romans at Jotapata. His hand may have been forced a little,

[1] *Life* 9, τὸ φιλογράμματον.　　[2] *Ant.* XX. 263.
[3] *Life* 10–12.　　[4] *Life* 13–16.
[5] στρατηγός, *B.J.* II. 562–8.　　[6] *Life* 29.

but that is not a complete explanation. Opposition from the Zealots, his own loosely-defined position as "ambassador", visions of himself successfully stemming the Roman advance— all these considerations probably contributed to his assuming a command which at the time was not officially his, and fighting with the Zealots, whom he really hated, against the Romans, whom he really admired. The inconsistencies in Galilee are partly due to Josephus' own character, which was ambitious, and even at times unscrupulous.

Josephus was not a fanatic: the hatred which the Zealots nursed against him, and his long stay in Rome, are ample evidence of this. His religion did not identify itself with a narrow nationalism. Although he was himself a priest, he was hardly what we should call religious; his life, so far as we can judge from his writings, was essentially worldly, and was not characterized by the exceptional spiritual fervour of one in union with Jehovah, whom he worshipped.

In a word, pride sums up Josephus as a man, and was his ruling passion. He had much of which he could justly be proud, but he let himself at times be carried away by it. "A priest and a Hasmonean" is a phrase frequently found in his writings, and no doubt was frequently on his lips. And to a Hasmonean, Herodian was the direct antithesis: the House of Herod was, in Hasmonean eyes, only half Jew, mere Idumean converts. This imagined superiority was responsible for many of the domestic troubles between Herod and Mariamne, herself a Hasmonean, and it was partly responsible for Josephus' shortcomings. It led him to despise other people who were not so well-born or gifted as he was himself.

He was a Pharisee, and, after his first visit to Rome, returned with a lively admiration for the Romans; he did not object to Roman rule, provided the Jews were given liberty to practise their religion. But after Jotapata, where he was taken prisoner by the Romans, he was used as an interpreter and mediator in the siege of Jerusalem; and then he was looked upon as a traitor to his country, an unprincipled coward serving only his own personal interests. The attack of Jonathan [1] must have been typical of the hatred felt against him. And although, strictly, his being a Pharisee did not thereby prevent him from having pro-Roman sentiments, yet this Pharisee, on his release when he came to Rome to live in a privileged position with Titus and Agrippa II, must have intensified that hatred which his fellow-countrymen already felt. For a time he may have disregarded it, but later there is some evidence for a change of views, or rather for an out-spoken expression of his true views. Josephus' last work is the most famous ancient apology for Judaism, and he was contemplating a work in four books on *God and his Essence*; [2] his first Aramaic *Jewish War* had been probably a semi-official Roman manifesto, directly inspired by Titus and Vespasian, and intended to prevent opposition to Rome in the East. A change did come over Josephus, and in this connection the death of Agrippa II was a momentous day in Josephus' life, because he now had no one out of respect to whom he felt bound to repress his sincere conviction. From this time probably date some of the seemingly inconsistent anti-Herodian passages in the *Antiquities*.

There is thus evidence for a change of view, because Josephus attempted to atone for the past in his writings. The persons with whom Josephus' ultimate views most nearly coincided were probably the Pharisees at Jamnia. Certainly the Zealots still hated him; the Sadducees would have little to do with a Pharisee, and a certain section of the Pharisees probably rejected pro-Roman views. But the Pharisaism of Jamnia, where, about the time of the edition of the *Antiquities*, the Canon of the Old Testament was beginning to be fixed, was of a revised type, and would not straightway reject Josephus because he lived under Roman patronage. The school of Jamnia demanded emphasis on the "peculiar" history of the Jewish nation, which was to be found in the *Antiquities* and the *Contra Apionem*; and Josephus himself was

[1] *Life* 424.   [2] *Ant*. XX. 268.

imbued with pride of race. Thus there are certain important points of similarity.

In the end, Josephus failed in what rather resembles an attempted palinode. The Jews did and still do reject him, but the reason is largely because the Christians took up Josephus' works owing to his short mention of Jesus in the *Testimonium*. In his lifetime, too, he does not seem to have been entirely successful. Even if he was in agreement with the school of Jamnia, he would only be in agreement with a small proportion of the Jews. Moreover, he had to think of his position at Rome, and his reputation with the literary circle of Epaphroditus, on which much depended. In this respect, the publication of Justus' *Jewish War* was critical for Josephus. His counter-attack in the *Life* was successful in its result. Thus he justified himself in the eyes of non-Jews, and especially Epaphroditus, and in doing so revived his earlier quarrels with the Jews. The new Pharisaism of Jamnia alone may have regarded him with favour because of his changed views, but even with them, apprehensive as they undoubtedly must have been of Christianity, the *Testimonium*, as Josephus probably wrote it, was long enough to arouse suspicion, and not long enough or bitter enough to win commendation from Jews. Josephus died hated by most of the Jews; but there are signs of growing appreciation of him. I. Abrahams says of him:[1] "Very unjustly, as it seems to me, Josephus has been censured for lack of patriotism, because he feared that the firebrands were more likely to injure Judaea than Rome. Josephus' faults are beyond defence, but lack of patriotism was not one of them. In real patriotism, loyalty to his people's spirit and pride in its institutions, no one, not even Philo, ranks higher." He was not generally appreciated in his lifetime, and only after his death by non-Jews. The statue set up in his honour at Rome,[2] and the indifference of his countrymen then and now, show wherein lie Josephus' success and failure.

[1] Schweich Lectures 1922, *Campaigns in Palestine*, p. 36.
[2] Eus. *Hist. Eccles.* III. 9.

From Josephus the man we turn to Josephus the historian, in an attempt to see how far his character influenced him for good or for bad as a historian. "His prejudices and idiosyncrasies", to quote Oesterley,[1] "make it sometimes necessary to use his evidence with caution."

As a historian, Josephus aimed at accuracy. His repeated assertions about his desire for truth show this. He mentions it in the introduction to each of his three works (*B.J.* I, esp. 9: *Ant.* proem., esp. 17: *Contra Ap.* I, esp. 3), and in the *Life* there is a still longer passage about it[2] in a digression on Justus. He knew the importance of evidence in support of a statement, as his list of decrees shows.[3] Even though lack of adequate authorities between *Ant.* XI and XV causes in the narrative a disproportion which in a work covering such a long period is much to be deplored, Josephus is never a mere plagiarist, because, while keeping very closely to his source, he imparts to it something which stamps it with his own individuality, and even tries to correct obvious errors. He is the main authority for the Roman period of Jewish history up to A.D. 70, and a very creditable one. Without Josephus' works, we should be very doubtful about the details of the siege of Jerusalem, and our knowledge of the rise of the Herods would have to be pieced together from coins and incidental references. Whatever is the origin or purpose of the long description of the murder of Gaius, and the accession of Claudius,[4] it is a recognized *locus classicus*, as also is the description of the tactics of the Roman army;[5] and his statements about Homer[6] inspired Wolf's *Prolegomena*. To appreciate the value of Josephus' works, we have to imagine ourselves without them.

The numerals in Josephus, which are frequently exaggerated and generally untrustworthy, are an unsatisfactory side of his work, but it cannot be said that their unreliability detracts

---

[1] Oesterley and Robinson, *History of Israel*, vol. II, p. 5.
[2] Esp. *Life* 329.   [3] *Ant.* XIV.   [4] *Ant.* XIX.
[5] *B.J.* II. 345 ff.   [6] *Contra Ap.* I. 12.

from Josephus' merits as a historian. The same applies to Herodotus, whose numerals are sometimes entirely fantastic, and to the books of the Old Testament, in fact to nearly all ancient histories, including that of Thucydides himself. Such unreliability is frequently due to manuscript tradition and not to the author.

Josephus' good faith as a historian cannot seriously be questioned, and in good faith he has made mistakes in detail on which critics are quick to seize. It is regarded as doubtful, for example,[1] whether his statement in *Ant.* XIX. 279 is true, for it assumes that Claudius knew of the outbreak when he sent the edict; the despatch of Nehemiah to Jerusalem in 460 B.C. (*Ant.* XI. 159–63) is questioned; *Ant.* XI. 303 —the end of Artaxerxes' reign—is inconsistent with *Ant.* XI. 304, dealing with Philip, King of Macedon, for there is an interval of one hundred years passed over without any comment; *Ant.* XIII. 301 gives an impossible date—57 B.C.—for Aristobulus' assumption of sovereign power.

There are also inconsistencies which can best be explained by the gradual change of view which can be seen in his character. Particularly is this the case with his attitude towards the house of Herod, signs of which appear also in *B.J.* II. 224–36, 314–53, 605. In all probability there was a second edition of the *Antiquities* published when the *Life* was added, and after the death of Agrippa II. It is the second edition which accounts for a passage like *Ant.* XVI. 395–404, an appendage to *Ant.* XVI, not in the Latin version, and containing adverse criticism of Herod, and for the two endings at *Ant.* XX. 259, 267. Laqueur [2] further emphasized Josephus' change of view between the composition of the *Jewish War* and that of the *Antiquities*, by comparing in detail *Ant.* XIV and *B.J.* I, which is certainly used as source for the account in *Ant.* XIV. The general statement that *Ant.* XIV gives more prominence to Hyrcanus than *B.J.* I. is proved—

---

[1] E.g. by J. P. V. D. Balsdon, *The Emperor Gaius*, p. 144, note 1.
[2] *Der jüd. Hist. Fl. Jos*, chap. 5.

Josephus even says Hyrcanus went to Egypt [1]—and moreover
Laqueur shows the very great number of divergences, particu-
larly in the first half of *Ant.* XIV, which imply criticism of
Herod, Antipater, and even the Hasmonean Antigonus.
(E.g., *B.J.* I. 223 = *Ant.* XIV. 277, which is contradictory:
B.J. I. 318 = *Ant.* XIV. 435, but with different implications.)
One of the most striking changes is that in *Ant.* XIV. 91 compared with *B.J.* I. 170: in the former Josephus substitutes
five συνέδρια for the five σύνοδοι in the *B.J.*, on the occasion
of Gabinius' visit to Jerusalem, but omits in the *Antiquities*
ἀσμένως, which appears in *B.J.* I. 92 (ἀσμένως ἐν ἀριστοκρατίᾳ
διῆγον).

Thus Josephus allows inconsistencies to stand in his works.
He may have intended to publish a second edition of the
Jewish War, incorporating his new views. (Laqueur indeed,
emphasizing *Ant.* XX. 267, makes much of this.) Certainly
another edition would not have caused Josephus much incon-
venience, and there are signs of changed views in *B.J.* II.
602–8, as if he started altering his early statements in the
Jewish War. Most of the statements in Josephus' works with
which it is impossible to agree, and which most strongly contrast with those elsewhere, are in the *Life*, e.g. 169, 373–80.
It is to be noted that the *Life* deals chiefly with his career in
Galilee, which he was defending after attack; the vituperation
is hardly different from that of a Cicero to a Clodius, a
Demosthenes to a Philip, a Caesar to a Cato, and the statements made through excess of over-wrought feeling are equally
untrustworthy. The revised account of his position in Galilee
given in the *Life*, brings up the question whether he was
guilty of "suppressio veri". Inasmuch as the *Jewish War* only
gives a part of the truth he was guilty to a degree, but it was
convenient for Josephus and adequate for the non-Jewish
public for whom his *Jewish War* was intended. So too with the
Testimonium. It seems certain that Josephus knew more about
the Christians than his short notice tells us, and that he, with

[1] *Ant.* XIV. 138.

most Jews, despised them. He maintained what has been termed a "stolid silence about Christianity",[1] and gives only a short account, suppressing some of the truth about them. He exhibited an equally stolid silence about the Synagogue, for the word is only used once by Josephus (in *B.J.* VII. 44; *Life* 280 has προσευχαί). But in works intended for Gentile readers, such silence is less surprising.

"Josephus is the Greek Livy." Such is Jerome's high estimate of him, implying that what Livy was to the Romans, Josephus was to the Greeks. Both wrote long histories, Livy from the foundation of Rome, Josephus from the Creation, and both histories have survived, as standard authorities on certain periods. Casaubon's estimate of Josephus is similar: "Auctor est in historia φιλαληθής, φιλόπονος, et multis eximiis virtutibus historico necessariis excellens, ut per me quidem provocare quemvis e graecis historicis. Illud excusare non possum . . ." (his treatment of Holy Writ).

But Josephus remains a Jew: his theme that God punishes the impious, and rewards the pious, is characteristic of this. In so far then as Jerome calls him the Greek Livy, the description seems perhaps not to do complete justice to Josephus— for he was not a Greek—or to the Greeks, whose "Livy" thus is a non-Greek. Josephus is a Jew who can "challenge any Greek historian" for painstaking care, good faith, interesting and instructive narrative; he may indeed be called the Jewish Thucydides. Nevertheless the personality of Josephus pervades all his works in a different sense from the personality of Thucydides. The retiring, enigmatic personality of Thucydides, typified in his laconic statement, "and it befell me to be an exile from my fatherland", is foreign to Josephus, who as a man was ambitious and whose besetting sin was pride.

Herein, the essential connection between the study of the man and of the historian reappears. Where Josephus lets

---

[1] Lightfoot, *St Paul's Epistle to the Galatians*, p. 366.

the unsatisfactory side of his character, the excessive pride of birth and race, born of ambition, gain predominance, his history suffers. In spite of the loud and frequent proclamations which he makes of the importance of truth (even in the middle of his narrative, e.g. *Ant*. XX. 156–7), there are occasions on which his narrative does not compare favourably with Thucydides or Livy. The hostile picture of Berenice, for example, in *Ant*. XX. 145–6 is not considered very credible; the favourable picture of the Herods in the *Jewish War*, and the less favourable one in the *Antiquities*, the two accounts of his "command" in Galilee in the *Jewish War* and the *Life*, the unnecessarily bitter attack upon Justus in the *Life*—all these passages, which have occasioned so much adverse criticism of Josephus, are directly or indirectly connected with Josephus as a man. Nevertheless, even if some of his statements are incredible, it is unfair to reject all his statements without careful consideration, and to despise him as an authority. Being proud, he was unwilling to confess failure, and he was liable at times to scorn the house of Herod and those connected with it. But even Thucydides the man prevails over the historian in the account of Cleon, and Josephus is not more unfair to the Zealots, for example, than was Thucydides to Cleon.

His faults as a man qualify his history, for where he talks of himself, and of events with which he has a strong connection, he is liable to fall short of the truth at which he aims: where Josephus the man is not put to the fore, his history is at its best and is worthy to be compared with that of Thucydides. To account for, and explain, his faults is difficult, but a clue may perhaps be found in the fact that Josephus was of Oriental Semitic stock, and Oriental peoples are in Western eyes sometimes capable of excess of feeling: hence his pride, due to excessive feeling about himself, and his bitter attacks on his opponents. Unless we can understand or feel sympathy with Semitic character, the true estimate of Josephus' character, and therefore of Josephus as a historian, may elude us.

The faults which we can pick out in Josephus are not the faults of an unprincipled scoundrel and a second-rate historian, because to maintain such a view is to be blind to everything else except his faults. Although, because of his obvious faults, Josephus cannot be called a great man, he is at least a great historian.

BIBLIOGRAPHY

This bibliography is not intended to be exhaustive. It contains details of the books referred to in the notes and text of this book, and indicates the wide fields of study opened up by the works of Josephus. Many of the books listed here have themselves bibliographies attached (e.g. Schürer: *A History of the Jewish People in the time of Jesus Christ*), which need to be consulted for a fuller picture of the literature directly or indirectly concerned with Josephus.

I. JOSEPHUS:

(a) TEXTS AND EDITIONS (arranged chronologically)

Hudson, J. *Josephi Opera.* Oxford, 1720

Cardwell, E. *Fl. Josephus de Bello Jud.* Oxford, 1837

Dindorf, G. *Flavii Josephi Opera.* Paris, 1865

Naber, S. A. *Fl. Josephi Opera Omnia* (Teubner Edition). Leipzig, 1888–96

Niese, B. *Fl. Josephi Opera Omnia.* Berlin, 1890–4

Reinach, T. (sous la direction de T. Reinach). *Oeuvres complètes de Flavius Josephus.* Paris, 1900–

Thackeray, H. St. J. *Josephus* (Loeb Classical Library). London, 1926–

(b) TRANSLATIONS

Whiston, W. *Josephus.* Edinburgh, 1737

Shilleto, A. R. *Josephus* (Bohn Library). London, 1900–3

Maynard, G. H. *The Works of Flavius Josephus.* n.d.

Williamson, G. A. *Josephus: The Jewish War.* The Penguin Classics, 1959

(c) ARTICLES IN WORKS OF REFERENCE

Edersheim, A. Art. "Josephus". *Dictionary of Christian Biography.* Ed. Smith and Wace. London, 1882

Hölscher. Art. "Josephus". *Real-Encyclopädie der class. Altertumwissenschaft.* Stuttgart, 1916

Thackeray, H. St J. Art. "Josephus". *Dictionary of the Bible,* ed. Hastings. Extra vol. Edinburgh, 1909

II. BOOKS AND ARTICLES DIRECTLY RELATED TO JOSEPHUS

Bloch, H. *Die Quellen des Flavius Josephus in seiner Archäologie.* Leipzig, 1879

Destinon, J. V. *Die Quellen des Flavius Josephus in der jüdischen Archäologie XII–XVII*. Kiel, 1882

Jackson, F. J. Foakes. *Josephus and the Jews*. London, 1930

Korach, L. *Über den Wert des Josephus als Quelle für die röm. Geschichte*. Breslau, 1895

Lacqueur, N. *Der jüdische Historiker Flavius Josephus*. Giessen, 1920

Richards, G. C., and Shutt, R. J. H. "Critical Notes on Josephus' Antiquities." *The Classical Quarterly*, vol. XXXI, nos. 3, 4, July–October 1937

—— "Critical Notes on Josephus' Antiquities", II. *The Classical Quarterly*, vol. XXXIII, nos. 3, 4, July–October 1939

Schmidt, G. *De Flavii Josephi elocutione observationes criticae*. Leipzig, 1893

Thackeray, H. St J. *Selections from Josephus*. London, 1919

—— *Josephus, The Man and the Historian*, New York, 1929

—— *Lexicon to Josephus*. Paris, 1930–

Weber, W. *Josephus und Vespasian*. Berlin, 1921

III. Books and Articles indirectly related to Josephus

Abrahams, I. *Campaigns in Palestine*. Schweich Lectures 1922. Oxford, 1927

Allegro, J. M. *The Dead Sea Scrolls*. Pelican Books, 1956

Balsdon, J. P. V. D. *The Emperor Gaius*. Oxford, 1934

Bevan, E. R. *The House of Seleucus*. London, 1902

—— *Jerusalem under the High Priests*. London, 1924

—— *Ptolemaic Dynasty*. London, 1927

Charlesworth, M. P. *Cambridge Historical Journal*, vol. 4, no. 2, 1933

Eisler, R. *The Messiah Jesus and John the Baptist*. London, 1929

Jack, J. W. *The Historic Christ*. Edinburgh, 1933

Jones, A. H. M. *The Herods of Judaea*. Oxford, 1938

Juster, J. *Les Juifs dans l'Empire romain*. Paris, 1914

Lightfoot, J. B. *St Paul's Epistle to the Galatians*. London, 1869

Madden, F. W. *Jewish Coinage*. London, 1864

Oesterley, W. O. E., and Robinson, T. H. *Hebrew Religion*. London, 1933

Swete, H. B. *Introduction to the Old Testament in Greek*. Cambridge, 1902

Tarn, W. W. *Hellenistic Civilization*. London, 1930

IV. WORKS OF REFERENCE

Bury, J. B. (ed.). *Cambridge Ancient History*. Cambridge, 1923–53
Bury, J. B. *Student's Roman Empire*. London, 1930
Ewald, H. *History of Israel*. London, 1876
Graetz, H. *History of the Jews*. London, 1891
Moore, G. F. *Judaism*. Harvard U.P., 1927
Mommsen, T. *Provinces of the Roman Empire*. London, 1909
Murray, G. *Ancient Greek Literature*. London, 1911
Oesterley, W. O. E., and Robinson, T. H. *A History of Israel*. Oxford, 1932
Schürer, E. *A History of the Jewish People in the time of Jesus Christ*. Edinburgh, 1910
Smith, G. A. *Historical Geography of the Holy Land*. London, 1904
Teuffel, W. S. *A History of Roman Literature*. London, 1873
Wright, F. A. *History of Later Greek Literature*. London, 1932

V. ANCIENT AUTHORS

(a) TEXTS AND EDITIONS

Dionysius of Halicarnassus. *Roman Antiquities*. Ed. Jacoby (Teubner Edition). Leipzig
—— E. Cary (Loeb Classical Library). London, 1922 ff
The Three Literary Treatises of Dionysius of Halicarnassus. W. R. Roberts. Cambridge, 1901
Nicolaus of Damascus. *Fragments*. Ed. Orelli. Leipzig, 1804
Plutarch. *Lives*. B. Perrin (Loeb Classical Library). London, 1914 ff
Polybius. *The Histories*. W. R. Paton (Loeb Classical Library). London, 1922 ff
Strabo. *Geography*. H. L. Jones (Loeb Classical Library). London, 1917 ff

(b) WORKS ON ANCIENT AUTHORS

Albert, K. *Strabo als Quelle des Flavius Josephus*. Aschaffenburg, 1902
Bonner, S. F. *Literary Treatises of Dionysius of Halicarnassus*. Cambridge, 1939
Finley, J. H. *Thucydides*. London, 1947
Lamb, W. R. M. *Clio Enthroned: a Study of prose-form in Thucydides*. Cambridge, 1914
Meyer, P. *Quaestiones Strabonianae*. Leipzig, 1879
Strachan-Davidson, J. L. Art. "Polybius" in *Hellenica*. Ed. E. Abbott. London, 1880

INDEX